GREEN LEAF
IN
DROUGHT-TIME

Jeremiah 17:8: *For he shall be as a tree planted by the waters, and that spreadeth out her roots by the river, and shall not see when heat cometh, but her leaf shall be green; and shall not be careful in the year of drought, neither shall cease from yielding fruit.*

GREEN LEAF
IN
DROUGHT-TIME

The Story of the Last C.I.M.
Missionaries from Communist China

By

ISOBEL KUHN

MOODY PRESS
CHICAGO

Printed in the United States of America

Contents

Foreword

GOD DOES NOT WASTE SUFFERING, nor does He discipline out of caprice. If He plow, it is because He purposes a crop. This book shares with us the secret of that purposing and lets us see something of the crop.

Peter counsels: "Do not be surprised at finding that that scorching flame of persecution is raging among you *to put you to the test,*" and the writer to the Hebrews assures us that "it afterwards yields to those *who have passed through its training,* a result full of peace." [1] So life apparently is meant to be a series of tests in the school of God. The tests He sends or permits are in reality His vote of confidence, for He undertakes not to allow us to suffer any testing beyond our powers of endurance. In those He permitted Arthur and Wilda Mathews to experience, they discovered His beneficent purpose, and transmuted them into occasions to bring glory to their God.

God staked much on the faith and uprightness of Job, and allowed Satan to test him to the limit in order to vindicate His confidence, rout Satan, purify Job, and edify Job's friends. Did He test these two children of His in China with similar ends in view— to show what He could be to His own when all other resources failed, to reveal the "secret source" of their "greenness"; to discomfit their enemies who found they could not starve God's children; to gloriously enrich and refine and temper their own

---

[1] R. F. Weymouth, I Peter 4:12; Hebrews 12:11.

lives, and to strengthen the suffering Chinese believers who witnessed their triumph?

This poignant story is written to the glory of God and to demonstrate what He can be to those who gladly embrace His will and accept His discipline, no matter how inscrutable.

—J. OSWALD SANDERS

Auckland,
New Zealand

Author's Acknowledgment

THE VOICE OF THIS STORY is that of Wilda or Arthur Mathews; I am only the pen that recorded it; with perhaps, a bit of experience in shuffling the narrative around until its pattern shows.

Miss Helen Dalton was the first to attempt the spadework. Arthur's letters were written in his minute hand, sometimes on airmail paper as thin as tissue. These she faithfully deciphered and typed for others of us to read more easily.

A real debt is owed to Mrs. Anne Hazelton, who first took up the task of organizing the letters and arranging the story. Her valuable work was cut short by the invasion of other responsibilities, so that for many months she was not able to work on it at all. The Mission, seeing no possibility of finishing it soon, gave the task to me. Already much of the arduous spadework had been done, and we give grateful thanks for it.

Others helped in various quiet ways. Miss Elsie Stelter worked hard at deciphering my penciled scribble, and typing it. My dear husband lent his frank and plain criticism, and also did many household chores to set me free for this work.

To all of these our grateful thanks; most of all thanks to Him, who wrought the inner miracles of this story. He is ready to work them again for any who will *take* His yoke and trust Him for the reason it is laid upon us.

Introduction

IT WAS JULY 23, 1953, when we first got the news. We were in Base Camp, Chiengmai, North Thailand, and in those hot countries houses are built more for airiness than privacy, so John's shout rang through every room.

"Dr. Clarke and Arthur Mathews are OUT! Safe in Hong Kong!" He had just received the telegram.

I was crossing through the back hall on my way to the kitchen, but I just stood where I was and shouted, "Praise God!" and from each room in the house I heard echoes of the same. Spontaneously we all lifted up our voices and sang, "Praise God from whom all blessings flow."

I do not believe that in all the years of our Mission history that the China Inland Mission, members scattered over the world in many continents, had ever so spontaneously lifted up a paean of praise with such *unity of heart*.

It was not just that these long-tried and much-tried brethren, held by the communists in the farthest corner of northern China, were now at liberty. It was that they were *the last of our C.I.M. family* to be delivered. Now we could say, "We, the largest Protestant Mission group in China, have all been brought through this Red Sea trial, and not one martyred." [1] Why such grace had been vouchsafed us, we could not say, but the paean of gratitude impulsively ascended to our great Giver of every good gift.

---

[1] Mr. Frank Parry was shot and killed at the beginning, but by robbers rather than communist activity, we believe.

I myself had slipped over China's back fence (so to speak) in 1950, and with our six-year-old son had refugeed our way through the jungles of Upper Burma to the nearest post of civilization; and from thence home to America. Mr. Kuhn had stayed behind to care for the hundreds of new converts who were turning to the Lord in those days of terror.

Safe on the shores of comfortable U.S.A. (I called it Behind the Plush Curtain), I watched the other members of our Mission, scattered in far places even to the Tibetan borders, as the Lord brought out one family after another. In January, 1951, the Mission had given that startling order for complete evacuation, 601 [2] adults and 284 [2] children to be brought from distant parts of China, simultaneously if possible, and conveyed home. Would the communists allow them all out? The funds for such an exodus—where would they come from? As we watched God's miracles take place (our husband and father was one, you know) those days, I felt like the apostle Paul wrecked on the shores of Malta. *They which could swim should cast themselves first into the sea* (that was Danny and I! We had had the opportunity to escape *and get to land*).

And the rest, some on boards, and some on broken pieces of the ship. And so it came to pass, they escaped all safe to land (Acts 27:43, 44).

Paul had been promised *all* should be saved. *Lo God hath given thee all them that sail with thee* (Acts 27:24)

We had no such promise to claim. But the inspired prayer of Mrs. Mason's, "Lord, may not a hoof nor a husband be left behind," had been

---

[2] These numbers do not include missionaries and children who had already withdrawn as far as Hong Kong.

claimed by many of us. The last two were *husbands*.

I am sure Paul was among those who could swim (had he not been formerly a day and a night in the deep without sinking?), so he would be among the first to get to land. As he stood there safe, and watched the terrible surf and the bobbing heads of those who could not swim, clinging to flimsy boards and broken pieces of the ship—what were Paul's feelings?

What were his feelings as he watched the struggles *of the last two?* The frightening roar and dash of the surf; the helpless little black dots now in sight as their board was lifted to a crest, now completely submerged as it sank out of sight in the sea-trough. As Paul watched the struggle of the last two I am sure he was in continuous prayer: "All, Lord! You promised that *all* with me should be saved! Even though they do not seem to be making any progress and they must be numb with *the cold* (Acts 28:2), I know they must be given strength to hold on. *I believe God!*" Did these words come with a sob from Paul's throat, in the moments when those last two *sank out of sight?*

For two years we had watched our last two, Dr. Clarke and Arthur Mathews (and for awhile Mrs. Mathews and Lilah, and Clarence Preedy), held by the cold and cruel elements of the Red Regime which deliberately tried to starve them. Sometimes they sank into silence, and we stood praying with sobs in our throats. Then again an unseen surge would fling out a letter and we would catch another glimpse of them, alive and still clinging. But most amazing of all was *their spiritual vigor.* Whence came it? Not from themselves: no human being could go through such suffering and come out so sweet and cheerful. Just read the contemporary writings of godless P.O.W.'s—bitter and cursing even when they had the grit to endure.

As I was in a small prayer meeting one morning Mrs. (Dr.) Joseph Macaulay prayed thus : "O Lord, keep their leaf green in times of drought!"

I knew in a moment that this was the answer. Jeremiah 17:8: *For he shall be as a tree planted by the waters, and that spreadeth out her roots by the river, and shall not see when heat cometh, but her leaf shall be green; and shall not be careful in the year of drought, neither shall cease from yielding fruit.*

That was it! There was an unseen Source of secret nourishment, *which the communists could not find and from which they could not cut them off.*

This is the story of that secret Source. To add another book to the many telling of trials under communist pressure is not necessary and is not our purpose.

But to tell of the secret Source by which a tree can put forth green leaves when all others around are dried up and dying from the drought—that is timeless. That is needed by all of us. Your drought may not be caused by Communism but the cause of the drying up of life's joys is incidental. When they dry up—is there, can we find, a secret Source of nourishment that the deadly drought cannot reach? This book wants to suggest an answer to that ageless question of suffering men and women.

> I will pour water on him that is thirsty,
> I will pour floods upon the dry ground;
> Open your heart for the gift I am bringing,
> While ye are seeking me, I will be found.
>
> LUCY J. RIDER

Part One

THE DROUGHT CREEPS UP

CHAPTER ONE

Thou, Lord . . . broughtest us into the net
—PSALM 66:11

"ARTHUR, IT IS BEGINNING TO SLEET! See how Lilah blinks her eyes when the wet snow hits her lashes."

"Yes, dear. This certainly is tough having to sit in an open truck in this weather, riding over the roof of the world—winter beginning at that. But that red snowsuit is keeping her snug. It is only thirty miles to Hwangyuan, so we won't be too long in getting there. That zipper opening at the bottom of the snowsuit works just right for changing nappies in the snow. I didn't know I had such a smart wife!"

Wilda Mathews smiled through the sleet that was falling faster now and cuddled her thirteen-month-old baby closer to her.

"Yes, I was fortunate to find such good, warm material in Lanchow. I made it plenty large too, so that she can wear it next winter also. Now that we are under the Red Regime one cannot tell what will be procurable in the days ahead." The old truck bounced and swung around a curve, causing all to hold on tightly to the nearest clutchable object. They were sitting on top of a load of goods, quite exposed to the storm and with no security of seat. This was truck travel in China in 1950, and not just one singular incident. It was past experience of such which

17

had caused the young missionary mother to think carefully into the needs of her little one and prepare accordingly.

"What gives me joy in this miserable sleet," went on Arthur, when a fairly straight road lay ahead of them and made speech possible again, "is the thought that we are on our way to do Mongol work at last! It just is unbelievable that with all the other missionaries thinking of evacuation to their homelands, we should be invited to do advance work! Invited by the Chinese church and O.K.'d by the communist government—if that isn't a miracle I'd like to know what is!"

"Don't you think the Reds O.K.'d it to bolster their propaganda of Freedom of Religion with the Hwangyuan church, as it was the church's request?" offered Wilda.

"Undoubtedly. But I see the hand of the Lord in this to get the Gospel to these long-neglected Mongols. He has put the burden of their unreached condition on my heart for years. I missed going to them when I enlisted in the army in World War II—patriotism got the better of me then. But now I feel God is giving me a second chance to evangelize the Mongols. That was my thought when I jumped at the invitation to Hwangyuan. Leonard Street knows it, and though as superintendent he felt reluctant to send us farther away from civilization at a time when common sense says to press closer to a place of easy exit, still one must have the boldness of faith to follow one's call. You remember the verse which came in my morning reading the day the passes came through? *In this thing ye believed not the Lord your God.* I was determined that that should not be said of us; especially of me when for the second time at a period of danger God opened a door for me to work among the Mongols."

Wilda said little for a time. The wind was icy cold and blew snow down her neck unless she huddled together just so.

"My feet are going numb," she murmured at last.

"I'm sorry, dear—try and wiggle them a little. Here, give Lilah to me. It won't be much longer now, and then we'll be *home*. They say that Plymires built a really lovely compound and all their furniture and books are still there just as they left them, expecting to return, of course. Weren't you told that we are to use everything and anything we want?"

"Yes, so they said. I'm thinking of that too. We ought to be very comfortable once we get there. They have a big foreign cooking stove, and an organ, and we are to have the whole section of their house, so it is just a matter of enduring this and then— welcome home! I wonder if the church will give us a feast? Of course they would in normal times, but they may not dare to show such a warmth toward the hated 'imperialists' now. Do they know we are coming on this bus?"

"Yes, I sent them word. Oh, look—isn't this Hwangyuan?" The truck was coming out of the steep-banked gorge now, and a little valley lay spread before them; and up on a foothill of the mountain nestled a small town. The flat-topped mud roofs, characteristic of China's great northwest province of Kansu, gave it the appearance of rows of mud boxes, interspersed with masts from which fluttered dingy tattered cloths—the Tibetan prayer flags. A mud or adobe wall encircled it, and as usual outside this was the Moslem suburb marked by its mosque. The river Sining was flowing swiftly by, and bare tall poplar trees on its banks stood black against the prevailing beige of road and mud hut.

In another few moments the truck had drawn up at the crossroads outside the city gate, which was too narrow for a bus to enter. Chinese of all classes were standing around watching, and mingled with them were other yellow-skinned peoples of variegated dress and headgears. As Arthur struggled to his numbed feet, and tried to help Wilda to stand on hers, he shot a few quick glances at the silent crowd, searching for the welcome committee. A few exclamations came when he lifted up the beautiful white baby in her scarlet snowsuit. Little Lilah was an Oriental's dream of loveliness—black curly hair, black eyes, and a very fair skin flushed to rose by the sting of the storm wind. Chinese hearts have always been tender toward little ones, and Lilah drew them irresistibly to her. But amid the murmurs of *hao-kan* (good to look at) there was no group who pressed forward with the smile which says, "She is ours! We invited her!"

A middle-aged man with a thin goatee had come forward, and a twenty-year-old Chinese lad stood beside him, but there was no joy on their faces.

"Ma Mu-shih?" (Pastor Mathews?) asked the one with the goatee.

Arthur had clambered down over the side of the truck by this time and had helped Wilda and baby to descend also.

"Yes," returned Arthur with his warmhearted smile. "And your honorable name?"

"I am Pastor Jen of the Gospel Hall," said the other, with a forced smile. But maybe this was just caution before so large an audience. It was not advisable, under the Red Regime, to show the least friendship toward an American or Australian. (Arthur is Australian and Wilda, American.) Arthur tried to catch this as a cue, and took the smile off his face, just bowing gravely.

"This is Samuel," went on the pastor, indicating the young man. Wilda remembered hearing that Samuel had played with the Plymire children in his and their youth, and so was almost like a member of the family. So she shot him an understanding smile, but there was no returning glint of appreciation. Truly Communism seemed to kill all joyous fellowship. Soberly they bowed to one another and then inquiries were made as to their luggage. Taking up the hand luggage, the two Chinese led the way into the city gate and through the cobbled streets to the long-looked-for compound.

All this time Arthur's quick eyes were darting here and there noting the motley nature of the population, for this little town was on the edge of the great Tibetan grasslands, not far from Lake Kokonor. The walk was not too long and the exercise was welcome to their cold, cramped muscles.

Soon they stood before an arched doorway marked in Chinese characters: GOSPEL HALL. Here they were met by a little group of Chinese. On each side of the entrance were rooms—that on the right occupied by Pastor Chin, that on the left by Pastor Jen. Beside Pastor Chin's room was a big building which, they were told, was the garage or luggage room.

Through the main gate they were ushered into a courtyard where stood the chapel, the clinic, the church kitchen, etc. Being accustomed to the Chinese style of architecture, Arthur guessed that the way through the church would lead them to the missionary's courtyard, usually the very back one, the most private of all. But first they were asked to sit down to a cup of tea and some bread in the chapel.

Once inside the compound walls, Pastor Jen whispered hurriedly to Arthur, "Just tell me what you want and I'll get it! Anything you want!" Much cheered by this, Arthur smiled back his thanks, but it soon appeared that Jen was not in charge of the compound. At tea a Dr. C—— appeared with two Chinese nurses. The communists, of course, demand that every human being "produce" something of a material benefit. Religious services are not considered a benefit to the community, so the church had undertaken the project of medical help and had registered with the government as a hospital. Chinese Dr. C——, therefore, considered himself as the head of the compound and acted as such. While they were drinking tea, a sound of sweeping in the inner courtyard made them guess that someone was preparing their rooms for them.

Sure enough, tea over, they were led through a gateway into the innermost sanctum. A large garden plot in the middle of a brick-laid courtyard contained a spruce tree, and behind it rose a two-story house with a balcony. Wilda noted its roominess with a sigh of satisfaction and relief. But what was this? Pastor Jen was not leading them to the center guest hall, but off to the side where stood the kitchen.

"You will occupy this," he said gravely, ushering them into the bare little room where stood a work bench and huge iron stove, and a child's rocking chair.

"And where do we sleep?" asked Wilda, whose quick eye had noticed that the large comfortable master bedroom was just overhead where the heat from the cooking stove would penetrate nicely.

"This way and I will show you," was the grave reply.

Horror slowly succeeded amazement as he led them outside the building, in through the center guest hall, then up the stairs which led out off it to a room at the farthest corner of the second story. It was entirely unheated and icy cold. It contained only two wooden beds and a built-in chest of drawers. Indicating these, Pastor Jen said apologetically: "You may use these tonight, but Dr. C—— wishes them for his hospital."

Thinking about her baby, Wilda asked, "What about the bedroom over the kitchen?"

"Dr. C—— and family occupy that," was the adamant reply. "The two nurses (my daughter is one) are in the bedroom next to it. This is all there is. Good night," and Pastor Jen had bowed himself out.

Wilda, still damp and cold from the snowstorm on the truck, turned panic-stricken eyes upon her husband.

"Arthur, there is something wrong here?"

His face was grim. "Seems like it, dear."

"They don't act as though they wanted us."

"I've never had such a reception in my life," he acknowledged.

"We were promised we would have all this inner courtyard to ourselves!" wailed the disappointed little mother.

"Yes, but you see, Dr. C—— is already in, and shows no intention of yielding up anything. We dare not press the missionaries' promise to us. We'll just have to take what they give us."

"But, Arthur," protested the poor young mother, still shivering from her icy ride, "just think what this

means! How can I care for my baby? She's got to
have a bath, and in winter that means I must wash
her in the kitchen where it is warm. Then every
single night must I bring her, fresh from her bath,
outside the house, through snow and storm, climb up
these stairs, and put her to bed in this ice-hole?
Arthur how *can* I?"

Her husband murmured, "One step at a time,
dear. Let's go back downstairs, and I'll light a fire in
the kitchen stove. I saw there was some coal there.
Then I'll go for our luggage and see what tins of food
I can find and a pot or so. Isn't it good that Lilah
isn't crying? How prettily she cooed at those two
nurses, and didn't they just love her! The Lord will
raise up friends for us, you watch. I can see that
Pastor Jen would have done more for us if he dared.
Under the surface he is sympathetic, I'm sure. Come
on downstairs. Let's organize as best we can. And
when Pastor Chin returns from Lanchow, after all
the welcome he gave us there, he ought to be a
help."

Night had set in as they lit a kerosene lantern and
proceeded to investigate the kitchen. Nearly half of
it was occupied by a pantry-arrangement of tiers of
shelves built to the ceiling and facing each other
across a narrow aisle. Pastor Jen had brought two
chairs, and Wilda sat on one with Lilah on the lap
while Arthur proceeded to light a fire in the stove.

"That huge thing is going to eat a lot of coal,
Arthur," said the young mother in anxious thought.
"It will take a wealthy pocketbook to keep that fed
in wintertime."

"I was thinking that myself," said her husband, as
he arranged some more coal on the crackling flames.
"Here is the Pastor. Maybe our trunks have come.
Do you mind sitting in the dark here while I take the

lantern and go see? Or perhaps I can find a candle."

"No, take it and welcome," said Wilda opening her damp coat to the comforting warmth of the big stove.

They do not remember what they ate that night. For Lilah they still had some Gerber Baby Food. Arthur had to see the luggage through customs and bring the cart back through the dark slippery streets. But as soon as possible bedding was spread out in the cold little upper room, and the three lay down in the dark, exhausted emotionally as well as physically. But first they had had prayer before blowing out the lantern. Stretched out, relaxed for sleep, they thought of the question again.

"Arthur, if they don't want us, why did they invite us? It was their letter that did it. We'd never have received the police pass to come if they had not written us that invitation."

"I've been pondering that, dear, and here is my guess. The Hwangyuan church is not C.I.M., you know. The pastors' salaries were always paid by the white man. I wonder if they did not think we would be able to help them with their salaries and also help them hold this huge compound. They asked if some other white missionary could be found to come and live here, and were told that we would like to—so they invited us. But in the interlude, between inviting us and our arrival, they have learned that if they accept a salary from the white man their lives will be in danger. So instead of an asset and security we have landed on them as a dangerous liability. We ought to pity them a bit."

"Well, is it all a mistake?" asked the weary young mother.

"Oh, no," exclaimed her husband energetically. "Remember that warning verse the Lord gave me the morning we got our passes! *In this thing ye believed not the Lord your God.* God may not have brought us here for the Chinese church, but there are still the unreached Mongols! Wasn't it thrilling as we passed through the streets this afternoon to see what a crossroads this place is! We've never had more wonderful opportunities to reach hitherto un-reachables. There are Tibetans, Mongols, aborigines, Moslems, Chinese—why it is endless! This place is strategic. I am sure that if the apostle Paul were here in our shoes, he would stick to the last breath of life in him. He was a strategist, and would see the Tibetans coming in here along roads from as far away as Lhasa and even India. Mongols too from all areas north and west of Kokonor; his heartstrings would feel the tug of these highways as they repre-sent the expansion routes for the Gospel. No, dearie, the Lord has brought us here. Let us rest our hearts in that and wait for Him to unfold His purpose."

And so with hearts stayed upon their Guide, and imagination fired with vision, the young couple fell asleep.

CHAPTER TWO

When Heat Cometh—
The Mongol Gospel Inn

A RTHUR WAS RIGHT about the Lord raising up friends. The next day a bright young face smiled in upon them and—two bronzed Mongol ones!

It was Ben ———, a graduate of Grace Bible Institute in Hangchow, who had come to the wild far places of his country as a home missionary. Only eighteen or nineteen years old, Ben was completely surrendered to the Lord, and eagerly sought the white missionary for counsel and fellowship.

He was staying in premises behind theirs with a Mongol teacher who had taught the previous missionaries. And his Mongol wife, Sengel, was all smiles and willing to serve Mrs. Mathews as she had the other missionary wife. We can imagine Arthur's joy at being able to start in again with his study of Mongolian (he had had a year of it already in Lanchow), and Wilda's happiness to have someone help share in the labors of primitive housekeeping.

Those first six weeks at Hwangyuan were cheerful with eager effort to serve the Lord. The very first Sunday Arthur was asked to preach in Chinese and did so, emphasizing the need for missionary work, for reaching out to those who had never heard. At the close of his message Pastor Jen asked for volunteers among the church members to go out in the

27

surrounding villages and preach the Gospel. Arthur put his hand up along with the Chinese Christians, but was hardly prepared for the next event. While an old Christian was organizing the volunteers into bands, Pastor Jen came up to Arthur and whispered in his ear, "You'd better not go." Then he deliberately arranged for one of the Christians to take Arthur visiting *in the town,* and to the homes of the Christians. That afternoon Arthur went but on his return talked it over with Wilda.

"It is obvious that the fear complex has gotten hold of Jen and the others," he said. "Evidently we are not to help the Chinese church evangelize, and Dr. C—— said he does not need my help in his clinic. You know Pastor Chin told us that they wanted us to do medical work—and here I've gone and bought a hundred dollars' worth of medicine just in response to his plea!

Spreading out his roots by the river may describe the Christian privilege of thinking through a problem in the presence of the Lord. As Arthur did this, an idea came to him. The Mongol caravans from Kokonor passed by the outside of the city wall where there were some houses. Why not try to rent one of these and set up a sort of caravan resthouse? The Mongols needed a safe place to leave their animals and pots while they went into the town to find a purchaser for their wool; also while they were buying the loads for their return journey—barley flour, cloth, iron pots, and such. Maybe Pastor Jen would know of a suitable place? So Arthur approached him.

"Yes," pondered the pastor, "that might be a good idea." And he knew of a Christian who owned a good-sized house right on the road. It had a large upper room over a courtyard big enough to accommodate camels—would Pastor Mathews care to go

and see it? Indeed he would and so the two set out.
The house was found and it was suitable; moreover,
the owner was willing to rent.

It was a happy missionary who hurried home to
his wife that night. "We've got it, dear!" he cried
out. "It is very suitable, though of course it must be
cleaned up and put into shape. I'm going to have it
whitewashed and then pictorial Gospel posters in
Tibetan, Moslem, and Chinese pasted on the walls.
Their bright colors will decorate as well as instruct.
I'm going to have a reading table, with literature in
all these languages, for more than Mongols will come
in. And now I know why I was led to bring in all
that medicine! We will have a clinic, and they can
get healing for body as well as soul!"

From then on every day was spent in fixing up
the Mongol Gospel Inn. He put in a board floor, had
a medicine cupboard made, and a big k'ang (bed).
Hopes ran high. One day he saw a Mongol boy,
talked to him, and found that he (Arthur) was understood! The laddie took him to his tent, pitched
out on the fields without the city walls, and in-
troduced him to his mother.

In the meantime two other young Chinese home
missionaries had joined Ben. These were Timothy
and John, and their bright young faith was a blessing
and stimulus to the Mathews' family. Wilda too was
going out visiting in Hwangyuan with the wife of
Pastor Jen. Little did she guess that her loving words
and smiles those days were to be the only direct
ministry she was to have among them. But it was
enough to show the native women and girls of
Hwangyuan that the white woman in their midst was
there to love them. Hudson Taylor used to say:
"There is a mighty power in *contact*. . . . They
are not clean, and sometimes we are tempted to draw
our skirts together; but I believe there is no blessing

when that is the case. . . . There is much power in drawing near to this people, and there is a wonderful power in *touching* people. A poor woman in Cheng-tu when she heard of Mrs. Riley's death said, 'What a loss to us! *She used to take hold of my hand,* and comfort me so. . . .' If you put your hand on the shoulder of a man there is power in it . . . there is something in contact: it is a real power we may use for God."

Those were days of the touch of the hand, the loving concern in the eyes, the simple testimony of the voice. They would not be forgotten later on when the government forbade it.

Arthur's whole soul was stirred and words ran into verse as they frequently did with him. He apologizes for using the first two lines of someone else's writing —they were his inspiration!

A Mongol: On my lonely steppes I wait
For the messenger of Christ, who cometh late.
The wild winds mock my despairing cry,
O, why don't they hurry; I die! I die!

The sun is fast sinking, the hour is late,
The servants of Christ, O why do they wait?
Lost and forsaken, and so my last cry
Quivers unanswered, neglected I die.

His servant: At my lonely post *I* wait
A messenger of Christ; pray not too late.
Would the wild winds could bear my heart's cry,
Christ died to save you, then why must you die?

The sun is fast sinking, the hour is late,
The servant of Christ at the fast-barred gate.
NO, not forsaken: O, Lord lead us on
In Thy blood-stain'd footprints, ere the daylight
is gone.

—R. A. MATHEWS

December 8, 1950, was the date set to open the Mongol Gospel Inn. The day before, a small boy came running to Arthur. "Chinese! A Chinese troupe have taken over your inn! They've moved in!"

You can imagine Arthur's feelings as he hurried to the spot and sure enough—the girls and young men of a Propaganda Troupe had spread themselves throughout his new rooms—and the *kang* hardly dry! He could not turn them out but indignantly protested. "You have no right here! It is I who paid the rent. I paid for the cupboard and the bed and everything here. What right have you to come and help yourselves to it?"

But the days of a just hearing were ended. It would have been wiser to have said nothing. The Chinese troupe did not remain in the Inn. Following Arthur's debacle with them, just the day before the place was to be opened, Pastor Jen himself came to Arthur and requested him not to go to the Inn again. "We Chinese will take care of it," he had said rather awkwardly.

On December 9 a policeman entered the Mission compound and strode up to their kitchen, calling for Timothy. When the latter appeared, he was roundly scolded for not having registered when he arrived in Hwangyuan, and then the officer of the law announced: "No one in this compound is allowed to do any village work without our permission. And the white people are forbidden everything, they may not have meetings outside this compound; may not give out tracts, may not dispense medicine. All their activities must be confined to within these walls"— and then he left.

You can imagine what a staggering blow this was to Arthur and Wilda. In fact, it was the fourth slap-in-the-face, so to speak, one right after the other.

The first blow was when Arthur was told that he was not to help with the medical work; the second, when he was not to evangelize in the villages outside the city wall; the third, when the Chinese pastor himself asked him not to go to the Mongol Inn which he had prepared with such labor and expense; and now the fourth, confined to the compound. What was there inside these walls to do? It just seemed as if every time they tried to do anything for the Lord, they were knocked flat! Life's accustomed joys were slowly drying up; but the trees of the Lord have a secret supply.

You will remember they had little furniture and practically no library. Plymires had plenty of each, and the possessions of other missionaries were in trunks in the luggage room also. One of the latter had written asking Arthur to open his trunks and send him something. So Arthur had gone to Pastor Jen with the letter and the two of them opened the luggage room. The lad Samuel, however, was immediately on the spot and, pouncing on the organ, said, "Plymires promised this to me!" He began to move it out for himself. Arthur, seeing that the opening of the trunks would be interpreted as a "help yourself" by the Chinese, wisely withdrew and refused to touch a thing.

And so we find them in their little kitchen with only a table, two chairs, and the child's rocking chair. In the corner they had put a locker trunk; Wilda covered it with a traveling rug and this became their prayer nook. Down on their knees before the Lord, *as a tree planted by the waters that openeth out its roots by the river,* they spread out their frustrations to Him whom they loved. They also spread out their bitter disappointment; to Arthur especially it was hard to see the door to the Mongols close. *And shall not fear when heat cometh but its leaf shall be green.*

Comforted by the Lord, they rose from their knees to see what could yet be salvaged from their Mongol dream. Arthur talked it over with Pastor Jen and decided to make the now-equipped building a base for forward work by the Chinese church! After all it did not matter who did the work as long as the Gospel was preached. And here were the three young Chinese home missionaries looking for an open door. "I would just stipulate," said Arthur, "that Ben, Timothy, and John be allowed to use it as their base too."

The three Chinese boy-missionaries were finding it difficult also. They were from the more civilized down-country provinces which fact was easily detected by their accent. Anything strange caused suspicion in those days, so the three lads felt a bit like foreigners too. More and more they sought fellowship and encouragement from Arthur and Wilda. Ben was especially close to their hearts.

The translation of his real name is Illustrious Benevolence, but that was too bulky for use in letters and certainly did not picture the eager-faced lad who was not yet twenty years old. It was easy for him to catch Arthur's enthusiasm for the need of the Mongols, and quick sympathy for the white man's frustration may have fired him on.

At any rate we find Wilda writing home:

> But the doors are opening for others, for young Chinese men and women who, having heard the call to service and received their training in Bible school or seminary, want to come into the harvest field in the great Northwest. . . .
>
> Ben has gone on to Tulan to fulfill his call to the ministry among Mongols. Slight of build and not robust in health, he has strong faith and courage

which he surely needs as he faces that work. Tulan is a very small place, twelve camel stages from here, with just a few Chinese homes centered around the post office and government offices. Scattered in the area around are possibly more than five thousand Mongol families, living in tents. It is to these Ben wants to go. Living is very difficult and expensive, and he is living by faith in a very real sense, for no group is behind him. He hopes to make a living by cutting hair. Mr. W———, a Christian shoemaker from this church, has gone to Tulan to be a witness there. I am sure you will remember these two men as they seek to spread the light under such circumstances.

Ben did not last at Tulan. His story is an epic for Chinese church history of faith, suffering, and apparent frustration. Before the end of the year he was back in the tender arms of Arthur and Wilda Mathews who, smarting from their own disappointments, knew how to comfort him with the comfort which they themselves had received from God.

And shall not fear when heat cometh but its leaf shall be green.

In a little while we hear that Ben (whose toes had been badly frozen on his return truck ride) was looking forward to the spring and another campaign to Tulan, this time knowing what he would face.

. . . its leaf shall be green; for a young Chinese home missionary as well as experienced foreign ones, the secret Source of life and comfort had not failed.

CHAPTER THREE

The Kingfisher Contends for the Prey

WILDA AND ARTHUR had decided to apply for exit permits to leave China. This was done, after much prayer, when the order came refusing them any ministry outside the compound, and they both had peace about it. This was increased when they learned that their letters advising the Mission of this decision had crossed one from Headquarters to them ordering them to evacuate, telling of the agreement that all the members of the C.I.M. should withdraw from China since it was clear their continuing presence was going to hurt the Chinese church and endanger it.

In their innocence they expected that their application to leave would be approved quickly as the Red government so obviously did not like them! Letters of the period hum with a happy note as they prepared for the long road journey out. One such ends:

Stop Press! Lilah has taken her first steps

Their interest in the salvation of the Mongols had not lessened, but events only corroborated the fact that God was not going to use them as the instrument. Dr. C——had been made head of the local medical association. Within a few days he had ordered the clinic in the Mongol Inn to be closed, and the Chinese home missionaries were told to find

35

rooms elsewhere. Arthur's stipulation that they were
to use it as a base was ignored. The boys were dis-
couraged, and one of them (John) decided to go
home. But Ben and Timothy started off for Kweiteh
and Hwalung for a time of ministry among the
churches there, always returning to Hwangyuan as
their base. Arthur felt sorry that the Chinese church
should not have helped these lads more, but executions had already begun, and everyone was in peril
of his life. Arthur wrote:

> The pastor told us today that when we go (they
> are getting prepared and know we cannot last
> here) then they are going to try to run a creche
> here for the soldiers' children. They know that
> the moment we go, the premises will go. Thus our
> work here and our value, as far as the church sees
> it, are to keep others from moving in here to live!
>
> We have tried everything with all our hearts,
> and had faith that the Lord would have something
> for use here, but He has shown us clearly that the
> doors are shutting *purposefully* at His willing, so
> with clear consciences we can think about trying
> the only door that seems open at the moment. We
> do not claim to be Pauls, but we can say that with
> the peace we have in our hearts about going now,
> the closing must be of the Lord and for His plans.
> Guidance is not easy at any time, and it very
> rarely comes in a hurry, only after a period of
> waiting on God, and then watching the circum-
> stances. The Israelites had to wait for the Ark to
> go two thousand cubits before they took a move,
> so they could see clearly the direction. That
> seems to be the safest policy on all matters like
> this.
>
> Just the other day we had a card from the lady
> in charge of the Melbourne Home, and she quoted
> this story: "Two small boys were playing soldiers.
> One said, 'There, I have all your soldiers sur-

rounded. Now what are you going to do?' The
other answered promptly, 'I'll ring up God'!"
That is about our position here, and we will rejoice that God is still on *the phone* as well as on
the *Throne*.

One of the government regulations for foreigners
leaving the land was that they register every single
article that they were taking out with them. And so
Wilda and Arthur began to sort their possessions,
selling everything that would not be needed on the
journey out. Down came the curtains, and even the
tablecloths were sold—all the simple pretties with
which Wilda's beauty-loving soul had tried to dress
up the barren rooms and make them homelike. In a
week or so they would be on their way, they thought,
and so they could do without table covers and china.
They retained only the tin plates, bowls, and mugs
which they would need to use on the truck journey
out. Wilda did keep her pressure cooker as she
meant to take that back to America with her.

A Russian family (Christians) had come into town
and they bought quite a few things, and Wilda gave
them still more, for as believers they were not popular with the Regime.

Their application for exit permits was filed with
the authorities on January 3, 1951. But day after
day passed and there was no indication that anything
was being done about it. It was not wise to ask—
they would be curtly put in their place, for the
Regime claimed to be perfection in its workings.

By February news drifted through of false accusations leveled against one of our missionaries in another place. Whenever there was one missionary
especially beloved by the Chinese, the communists
trumped up the vilest of accusations against him or
her. (A case in point was their false denunciation

and murder of the beloved Dr. Wallace in Canton.)
Arthur learned that the accused missionary, among
other things, was charged with immoral treatment of
women servants. This he took as a warning. On
February 18 Arthur went to his wife:

"Wilda, Sengel will have to go. Sorry, but we cannot afford to have her presence in the kitchen, when
I am lighting the morning fires, used to besmirch my
character. I'd rather be maid-of-all-work than have
such lies trumped up against me!" Daily he had had
morning prayers in Mongol with the teacher and his
wife, Ben often joining them. They were professedly
Christians but now that the missionaries were to
leave, there was no point in their continuing to study
Mongolian any longer. So the two were called in
and in a loving, friendly way, the severance was
explained, and they decided to go—back to Sining.
Thus the compound was shorn of two more friendly
faces.

Still no reference was made to their exit. Toward
the end of February Arthur wrote his parents:

> With our feelings inside like stretched rubber,
> we do not find it easy to write letters. You know
> the feeling, and I can guess that you are a bit that
> way yourselves even now. It's the old top-knot
> that feels it most, but even for that we have a
> promise, *Thou wilt keep him in perfect peace
> whose mind* [imagination] *is stayed on thee.* The
> imagination is what jumps around into all sorts of
> places that it ought to keep out of. One day we
> are as bright and cheery as crickets, and the next
> as down as it is possible to be. . . . The tempta-
> tion keeps coming to think that our *way is hid
> from God,* but we know He cares and plans.

On March 8 there seemed to come a break. A
government official from the Central government had

arrived who was to inquire into the applications for exit of all missionaries. They nicknamed him the Kingfisher, from the character which represented his surname. Now things would get along! Arthur was summoned to the police station for an interview.

A few days before, they had received a letter from one of our Mission directors saying:

> I've just signed a paper which you will all be signing soon I presume. . . .

They did not know what he referred to, but when Arthur appeared before the Kingfisher, this gentleman appeared very friendly. He explained his purpose in coming and asked Arthur if he would sign a paper which was a petition for world peace. "Oh," thought Arthur, "this is it! I am for world peace most certainly"; and without further contemplation he put his signature to it.

The Kingfisher looked pleased and then said, "Now what contribution are you ready to make for world peace? You have signed a petition for it. I would suggest that since you were in India while you were in the British army, that you ask your Mission to send you there as a missionary. We would give you an alphabet number, say Mr. *X*, and, once a year or so, you could make secret reports to another, say Mr. *P*. Both you and he will be carefully guarded as to your identity, and it is just a little matter of helping forward the cause of peace."

In a moment Arthur saw the trap into which he had been led. By *world peace* Kingfisher meant a world conquered and dominated by Communism. And this was an invitation to become a fifth columnist in India! The Kingfisher smilingly hinted that once this arrangement was made, their exit papers could be arranged quickly. Aghast Arthur began to back away cautiously, not absolutely sure that he understood the proposition and not willing to give offense until it was necessary. He was told to go home and consider it and come back the next day with his answer.

On his way home, Arthur saw, pasted on the city walls, large notices with red checks through lists of characters. They were the names of those who were to be executed the next day—those who would not co-operate with the Regime! Now it was, that imagination did indeed "jump around into all sorts of places." If he were killed, what would happen to his lovely wife and baby toddler? He shuddered. Years later he was to say. "I wonder if Daniel's three friends had a little girl at home with sweet, pure face and small trustful hands? When they chose the fiery furnace, did they leave a wife behind them, unprotected?"

He never for a moment thought of consenting; he was just in the "midnight of fear." Awakened in a depth of night we have only half a grip on ourselves and fear can inflate itself and torture us.

Hurrying home, he told his story briefly. They ate supper; he carried his little girl up to her cold faraway bedroom; then came back to Wilda.

"Dearie, what made you sign so quickly? Without giving it a thought?"

"Mr. Sinton's letter saying he had signed. I wonder what he did sign. It could not have been this. Oh, what a fool I was!" And you can imagine the despair. Drought had brought the forest fire and the flames were licking toward these two young trees of the Lord's planting. What chance was there for survival? . . . *that spreadeth out its roots by the river.* Water is the thing that conquers fire. So down on their knees by the little old trunk in the kitchen

corner went the two, and they read the Scripture.
Psalms 140 to 144 fell open before them.

Deliver me, O Jehovah, from the evil man 140:1
They have set gins for me   140:5
When my spirit was overwhelmed
within me
Thou knewest my path
In the way wherein I walk
Have they hidden a snare for me   142:3
Bring my soul out of prison that I may
praise thy name   142:7
Make haste to answer me, O Jehovah;
my spirit faileth   143:7
Blessed be Jehovah, my rock   144:1
Who teacheth my hands to war
And my fingers to fight . . .
Rescue me and deliver me out of great
waters   144:7
I will sing a new song unto thee, O God 144:9
He riddeth my way perfect   II Samuel 22:33
                              (Hebrew, lit. marg.)

The next morning Arthur was summoned again.
Not knowing if it would be prison or death, he kissed
his wife and little one, put a *Daily Light* in his
pocket, and kept praying Psalm 141:3: *Set a watch,
O Lord, before my mouth. Keep the door of my lips!*
The Kingfisher had a sardonic smile for him.

"You signed the World Peace Petition thinking
we'd let you go if you did—didn't you? You're a
hypocrite. Come now, just what contribution to
world peace are you willing to make?" And then
the gruelling questions, suggestions, innuendoes for
some three hours.

"I cannot do these things you ask," Arthur argued
patiently in a later interview. "The Bible says I may

not." Arthur knew that the Kingfisher had once attended an English Bible class in a different city under a C.I.M. missionary and that he was somewhat acquainted with the general story of the Gospel.

"Where does it say you may not?" demanded the Kingfisher. "Show me!"

Delightedly Arthur went home and got out a New Testament to present to the man. But first he marked it carefully. When he brought it the next day, it was simply put aside, and later as he was leaving the police station, a guard thrust it at him contemptuously—"Here!" And that was the end of that.

Going home each afternoon he saw the people crowding out of town to the execution grounds. Everyone was forced to attend and observe, school children included. Every day new names were posted. Back in the compound, Wilda, hearing the shots, would wonder whose soul was being spilled into eternity now? But they had agreed that they would never comply.

For seven long days Arthur was called to go through this daily, always the Kingfisher holding up to him a quick and easy exit if he would compromise just a little bit. *Incline not my heart to any evil thing . . . let me not eat of their dainties,* was his prayer. And every night of that long week the husband and wife went to the little trunk and read Psalms 140 to 144 in the presence of the Lord. . . . *spreadeth out its roots by the river,* and nightly their heated fears were cooled and they were helped.

But it could not go on forever. There came a day when the Kingfisher handed him a long questionnaire dealing with all matters relating to "change of thought" and reasons for renouncing imperialistic thinking and Fascist totalitarianism. Then he was given the names of five of his fellow missionaries

and told to write a report on them. This was the
final showdown. Arthur took it home, and together
the two young missionaries asked God for the right
words. Arthur's life was at stake, they imagined.

"What contribution are you prepared to make to
the cause of world peace?" asked the paper. Arthur
wrote: "I believe that the Gospel of Jesus Christ is
the greatest power for peace in this world and my
best and only contribution to the cause of world
peace will be given as a minister or missionary of
the Gospel."

To the reports on his fellows Arthur wrote glow-
ingly all the good things he had ever heard. A Chinese friend happened (? or was sent by God) in and
found what he had done.

"Oh, you had better not give them that," he exclaimed anxiously. "You see they can erase your
words and write in a vile charge and—there is your
signature at the bottom of it!"

Arthur started back in horror. "Well, if that is
what they do," he cried impulsively, "into the fire
this goes," and, suiting the action to the word, he
stuffed the report into the fire. Leave-taking the next
morning was solemn. That the Kingfisher would be
angry went without saying, and the daily executions
were still on. We can imagine the feelings of husband and wife as they parted, and Arthur took his
weary way over to the police station.

"The papers?" said the Kingfisher, and Arthur
handed over his contribution to world peace state-
ment. It drew a scowl.

"Do you know —— ——?" the Kingfisher shouted, naming the missionary against whom charges had
been laid.

"Yes."

"He thinks he's going to get out of China, but he

won't! I've sent word to every port to stop him." The blast of hatred made Arthur shrink, but at the same moment he had to quickly drop his eyelids lest the gleam of exultant triumph be seen. For he knew that this missionary *was already out*. *Under his feathers shalt thou trust*. The Feather Curtain of God had fallen so lightly and silently around His child that the Kingfisher had not yet heard that he had lost his prey. But that knowledge put new courage into Arthur to stand and endure the next assault.

I will pour water on him that is thirsty; yea, the tree of the Lord is often secretly refreshed to the puzzlement of man who can only see how parched is the outside.

"Where is your report on the five missionaries?" thundered the Kingfisher.

Arthur straightened his shoulders, "I am not a Judas. If you expect me or anyone else in the China Inland Mission to do that kind of thing, you had better not try because we cannot do it. To do as you ask would be treason to the cause of Christ."

"The Central government has given me the authority to issue your road-pass if everything was satisfactory," he said slowly. "What a pity you wouldn't co-operate. A little matter has arisen. Someone has made charges against you, and they must be investigated. *And investigations take a long time*. You may go home." And that was the last they heard from the Kingfisher: he left for Peking and did not come again.

Wilda must have been overjoyed to see Arthur walk in that night; at least he was home and not in prison or on the execution grounds. But after they had put the baby to bed and went to the corner to kneel by the little trunk, their desperate plight swept over them. Two little grains of sand they seemed, surrounded by millions of hate-breathing communists, so very far from the coast. Hundreds and hundreds of miles between them and the nearest Chinese port. They were to be accused, and no one willing to investigate the truth. It was two despairing hopeless human beings who raised their cry that night. "Lord, speak to us!" And He did.

Their Bible opened at Isaiah 49:25: . . . *the prey of the terrible* SHALL BE DELIVERED: *for I will contend with him that contendeth with thee, and I will save thy children.*

Arthur and Wilda rose happily to their feet, their hearts bubbling over with joy. "We have his promise," said Arthur, "we are not the prey of the terrible. We are the prisoners of the Lord Jesus Christ—just lent to evil men to show forth the abundance of His power! Our days are on deposit with Him; let Him hand them out to use as He will."

And so in the midst of that scorching drought the little trees put forth tendrils of green leaves of faith in His Word, and they claimed His promise to be delivered.

The next Sunday Arthur was asked to give his testimony in the church and he took the burning bush as his theme. "You will be burned but not consumed," he told them, and gave his experience with the Kingfisher and God's answer of Isaiah 49:25. Unknown to him, it was his last message to the Chinese church. There could not have been a better one—*green leaf in drought* was all the way through it.

> My cloud of battle-dust may dim
> His veil of splendor, curtain Him;
> And, in the midnight of my fear,
> I may not feel Him standing near.
> But, as I lift mine eyes above,
> His banner over me is love.
>
> —GERALD MASSEY

CHAPTER FOUR

Faith Goes Into the Pressure Chamber

HOW GOOD IT IS that our salvation does not depend on our feelings! The Lord *is* near whether we feel His presence or not. Christ's blood *is* sufficient for our sin's debt whether we "feel" the flush of glowing faith or are shaken with fears. Because human feeling often goes into sudden revulsion. Passion can unexpectedly turn to hate, as the story of Amnon and Tamar so truly reveals.

In the exultation of God's quick and definite assurance of deliverance Arthur and Wilda did not notice that He had not said *when*. It was to be a full two years for the one, and even longer for the other, so God in His mercy had been silent on that point. But as days passed and there was no sign of the promised deliverance, faith was tested.

Our tests, like our crosses, are different, each being suited to our particular need. Arthur's test was fear; fear of what would happen to his dear loved ones, if he were taken from them. The promise of deliverance quieted that.

But to Wilda the test was *doubt*. Was this God's doing, or were they the victims of a mistake? Were they in God's hands only, or was Satan manipulating their affairs? It was the old problem of what is called, theologically, "second causes."

If only the Hwangyuan church letter of invitation had not come! Word began to come of fellow missionaries being released and getting home. They might have been among them, if they had not come to Hwangyuan.

If only Arthur had not signed that petition for world peace, the Kingfisher's hopes of converting him to Communism might not have been raised, he might not have "lost face" and maybe might have released them. Why were they sent to such a poor place as the kitchen and faraway bedroom? Why were doors to service allowed to be closed?

At least, if they were to stay in this place, why hadn't God warned them so that they would not give away all their outfit? The bare windows, the bare table boards, the tin mugs and bowls seemed sometimes like the last straw. Why? Why? Had they made a mistake to come, or hadn't they?

When a child of God makes a wrong choice, does he step out of the favor of God and so is outside the circle of His power to control his affairs? Does he step into the hands of Satan to become the victim of his malicious teasing and torturing? These age-long questions will assault any honest Christian who is seeking to follow the Lord. And any honest reader will not criticize but only bow his head in humble sympathy as he watches this young missionary in the crucible of doubt.

March 25, 1951, Wilda always remembers as Black Easter, for it was that day when she struck bottom, so to speak. It was during that final service with the Chinese when the leader asked them to sing, "He Lives," and suddenly Wilda found she could not sing. If He really "lives today," *why* had He allowed this? Opening her lips with the congregation, no song came. It was an appalling moment for a missionary. The drought had dried up outward comforts and freedom; was it to be allowed to kill the roots which needed to spread out to the river?

It can attack them, but if the young tree steadfastly reaches out toward the Water of Life, the drought and even the forest fire will be driven back.

Alone in the bare kitchen amid her drab tasks Wilda suddenly remembered two tracts, one which Miss Jessie Hunt of California had sent her the previous autumn and one from Miss Helen White formerly of Biola. One was by A. B. Simpson entitled, "The 'If' in Your Life." The other was by Hudson Taylor on "Second Causes."

"If only that letter had not come, inviting us here." What about the "if"? She got them and read: " 'Lord, *if* thou hadst been here, my brother had not died.' And He could have been there; He was not far away. He knew all about it, *and He let him die.* I think it was very hard for that woman. . . . I have come to think that there is an 'if' in every life. . . . It is something that God could have made different, if He had chosen, because He has all power; and yet He has allowed that 'if' to be there.

"I do not discount the 'if' in your life. No matter what it is. . . . Come to the Lord with your 'if', and let Him say to you what He said to Martha. He met her 'if' with His 'if'! *Said I not unto thee that IF thou wouldst believe, thou wouldst see the glory of God?* The glory of God is to come out of the 'if' in your life. . . .

"Do not be thinking of your 'if.' Make a power out of your 'if' for God. . . .

"Do you know that a light is to fall on your 'if' some day? Oh, glorious horizon! Then take in the possibilities and say, 'Nothing has ever come to me, nothing has ever gone from me, that I shall not be better for God by it. . . .'

"Face the 'if' in your life and say, *For this I have Jesus.*"

Little root . . . seek the river!

Wilda did. The second tract said: "The secret of Hudson Taylor's rest of heart amid such tempests of hate was his refusal to look at second causes. . . . He believed it was with God, and God alone, he had to do." When his dear wife died, Hudson Taylor wrote, "If satisfied with His will and way, there is rest."

Turning to the Word itself the Lord gave Wilda II Chronicles 20:17: *Ye shall not need to fight in this battle: set yourselves, stand still, and see the salvation of Jehovah with you.*

Also Ruth 3:18: *Sit still, my daughter, until thou know how the matter will fall.* Tender words, for our Lord never scolded Martha for her "if"; nor Mary (who accompanied the same "if" with mute worship, prostrating herself at His feet), but with her, He wept. Wept at the sorrow which must accompany spiritual growth in our lives: for by suffering He also learned obedience.

Two weeks after her "Black Easter" we find Wilda writing:

> I know you are praying daily for us in this our severe testing time as we pray for you in your testing. The heart conflict has been terrible but peace and quiet reign in both our hearts now. We can only follow Naomi's advice and *sit still*, trusting all things to work together.

That Arthur was standing by his wife and searching the Scriptures with her is evidenced by his letters. He writes:

> At first all our thoughts were on getting out, but now our thoughts are all on getting out of these days all the hidden gold that the Lord has laid up for us. So in the first days we were at the

mercy of the Egyptians, and they could do what they liked with us, and we would react with greater distress and *wonderings*. . . .

Psalm 66:10-13 was given to them at this time. *For thou, O God, hast proved us: thou hast tried us. . . . Thou broughtest us into the net. . . . Thou hast caused men to ride over our heads; we went through fire and water: but thou broughtest us out into a wealthy place.*

> *Thou didst it* is the text that I have before me these days [he continued] and so we refuse to question, or complain even though the days may seem to have no sense in them. THINE *hand presses me sore.* . . . Not Haman's Pharaoh's Herod's or Pilate's, but Thy hand!

And again:

> These trials of faith are to give us patience, for patience can only be worked as faith goes into the Pressure Chamber. To pull out because the pressure is laid on, and to start fretting and thinking that God doesn't understand what He is doing, would be to lose all the good He has in this for us. "When we learn to kiss the rod," Spurgeon says, "then He burns it. When we are still, then the rod is still." I think that both of us can say that we have been enlarged these months.

When unjust and unfair treatment aroused the natural heat of resentment, came this from Alexander MacLaren: "Meek endurance and meek obedience, the accepting of His dealing, of whatever complexion they are and however they may tear and desolate our hearts, without murmuring, without sulking, without rebellion or resistance, is the deepest conception of the meekness which Christ pronounced blessed." And, "The meaning of all that God does with us—

joys and sorrows, light and darkness . . . is that our wills may be made plastic and flexible."

Wilda looked back on this experience of *faith in the Pressure Chamber* as her "lye bath." When she was a young girl, she had worked for a summer in a fruit canning factory. The fruit was plunged into a lye bath to skin the peaches, then washed and brought to the workers on belts. They then packed it into tins ready for canning. Wilda's skin is very sensitive and for months after she had finished that work and was back in school, her hands still kept peeling—lye works so thoroughly that layers had to come off a long time after. And so with this crucible experience. The layer of *looking at other causes* had to come off; then the layer of quickness to anger in the heart; the layer of longing for pretty things; the layer of oversensitiveness; the layer of impatience (can't we go *now?*); the layer of mere submission, and so on.

On *April 10, 1951,* Arthur wrote:

> . . . Spring is just starting—no green yet, but it is trying hard. I'm still in my wadded camel-hair gown. We are living on the "fat of the land" —spinach dried right out, and carrots that look and peel like good old iron-barks. Thought we would be off earlier so went through all our bottled fruit and tomatoes, rather than leave them for others to enjoy, but then complications arose so here we comfortably sit. Still floating, praise the Lord.
>
> If we were to believe all we hear the commies say just now, it would appear that all the dirty rotters in the Mission were in the Northwest! Funny (?). Of course you and the home folk know us, so we are not worried. We need to be Christian, Pliable, and Obstinate, all rolled into one. Pliable in the Lord's hands, Obstinate in other quarters, and Christian to the church and

the world. We are learning, *Who art thou, O great mountain?* The stand we are taking is: *before Zerubbabel thou shalt become a plain.*

Wilda feels the altitude (9,500 feet!) and cannot overdo things. Lilah fortunately has no worries apart from the lack of "high" eggs. She got used to the highly flavored ones (storage eggs) during winter (the rest of us had to use respirators!) and cannot enjoy the fresh ones coming in.

The church is co-operating well among themselves and we hope they know what they are doing. When the time comes for us to leave, it will be a case of "unswept, unhonored, and unsung" as far as we are concerned.

Pray on for us *all*, that wherever and in whatever circumstances, it may be true that for us to live is Christ. That's all that matters. Wonder if Eric is still there—he may remember Leah and her friends; they are *Alexander the coppersmith* all over again.

Kindest regards,

ARTHUR

It was in the next months that Arthur, again inspired by the first two lines of someone else's thought, penned the following:

In the center of the circle of the will of God I stand,
As I launch from sheltering harbor to obey His last command.
What though waves o'erwhelm my vessel, and grim fears my faith assail,
Still I'll stay upon His promise, for that cannot, will not fail.

In the center of the circle of the will of God I stand,
Where the warfare wages fiercest, 'tis the place that He has planned.

Though dread foes may storm my castle, and the
    battle seem but lost,
I will claim in Him the vict'ry, and hold on
    whate'er the cost.

In the center of the circle of the will of God I
    stand,
There can be no second causes, all must come
    from His dear hand,
When dark clouds obscure my vision, and the way
    I may not see,
I will trust Him in the darkness for I know He
    pilots me.

In the center of the circle of the will of God I
    stand,
Though the universe around me shows small trace
    of His dear hand.
Yet in darkness as in daylight, in the gloom as
    sunshine fair,
I will trust Him for His presence, for I know He's
    always near!

It was their answer to the Pressure Chamber. **And
they** sang it to the tune of "There's a Light upon **the
Mountains"** [1] in the days ahead, for the drought **was**
to increase. But this leaf stayed green all **the way**
through.

---

[1] *Keswick Hymnal,* No. 384.

CHAPTER FIVE

"'Thou'rt God,' When I Can't Understand"

I T WAS ONLY A WEEK after the Easter message when Pastor Jen came to Arthur and told him it would be better if they did not attend church any more. Spies of the Red government usually came to church services to find something with which to accuse the Christians (all over China this was the policy), and as the charge leveled did not have to be important, it made each Christian nervously scan his smallest complications. We write this to excuse the church's weakness. No one should criticize them who has not *sat where they sat*.

For instance, "the little matter that had arisen," to quote the Kingfisher, and which he used to detain the Mathews' family, were the following charges made by Leah, a female Diotrophes in the previous station, who acted as spy for a Mrs. Kao whom they had never met.

Arthur was accused:

1. Of standing on a table belonging to the church.
2. Of misusing a memorial plaque which had been given Dr. Kao.
3. Of killing a dog.
4. Of locking the kitchen door of the church.
5. Of closing the school at Changyeh.

There was truth in each of these charges. The table was rickety, and the church had allowed the use of it. The dog was a stray, and the deacon asked him to kill it. The kitchen door and the school were matters decided and agreed upon by a church meeting with the proper leader present, and Arthur was asked to carry out their wishes. Arthur's signed confession of each of the above charges was a masterpiece of groveling. The serious-minded communists would see in it good material for antimissionary propaganda, but not so the foreign reader. The Lanchow missionaries had many a hearty laugh over the hidden sarcasm in the abstruse wording. It was finally arranged that Mrs. Kao should be paid three million Chinese dollars to comfort her! (That would be about $135.00 U.S.)

Under such a Regime the less contact you had with the foreigner, the better for you—hence the church's request. But to Arthur and Wilda it meant they were cut off from spiritual fellowship with the Chinese brethren. From then on they had longer family prayers with singing every night in the kitchen, and special sessions on Sundays.

The next month (May, 1951) they were granted the use of another room upstairs which was not quite so hot, as the summer approached.

Then in the middle of July word came that the Sining missionaries had all been granted exit permits (except Clarence Preedy) and were leaving. Along with this came secret word to them to get ready to go also. As Wilda's mother and father had both been ill (heart attacks) they jumped to the conclusion, naturally, that God was going to send them home so that the grandparents would get to see dear little Lilah, who, of course, had never met them. They packed everything and even went to eat with the

Chinese for four days, wishing to be fully ready at
split-second notice. But as no further word came,
they realized it was only another tantalization, so
came back to the kitchen and unpacked.

Wilda writes:

> Right after I last wrote, there was a sudden flut-
> tering of our hearts' wings and they soared high
> for a short spin, only to make a forced landing
> in more mud. So life seems to go. Our times are
> still in His hands though, and when His time ar-
> rives, there will be no more mud holes! Peace
> took wings too, for a few days, as we looked to
> man. Now that our Father has been able to get
> our eyes centered upon Himself again, once more
> peace is reigning. . . .
>
> Two words sum up these two weeks—packing
> and waiting. Everything is packed. I even get
> Lilah's clothes each day (clean ones) out of the
> road suitcase. We've been eating with others be-
> cause our utensils are packed. Can't go on like
> that for long though, so we are making other ar-
> rangements. It seems the "last straw" but by
> God's grace must not "break the camel's back."
> Another party has moved forward, but one has
> become a Peter. May he soon meet Rhoda.
> [Friends at home recognized that reference to
> Dr. Clarke's being sent to prison.] We feel for
> you in all in this disappointment as much as for
> ourselves. But God is able and we do believe to
> see His goodness. We wait only upon God.

That last was a reference to Psalm 40:1 which the
Lord had used to bless them in this trial. "I waited
patiently" in the Hebrew means, "in waiting I
waited." So Arthur was led to pen these lines (another green leaf from a dried-up hope!) :

In waiting I'm waiting for Thee, blessed Lord,
Though encompassing foes threaten ill:

My weak, trembling faith clingeth fast to Thy
  Word,
And trustingly waiteth Thy will.

In waiting I'm waiting for Thee, Lord, alone—
Not deliv'rance from dangers without—
For Thyself, Lord, to come and claim my heart's
  throne
And self's lesser hopes put to rout.

In waiting I'm waiting my hope bruis'd and sore,
Murmurs, Lord, at Thy "tarrying yet";
Thou plannest a harvest where death locks the
  door,
Then grant, Lord, my faith ne'er forget.

In waiting I'm waiting Thy fire, Lord, to burn
The base metal that quails 'neath Thy hand;
To *be still and know*—through Thy fire would I
  learn
"Thou'rt God," when I can't understand.

He did not know as he laid down his pen that that
very month, death was locking the door on Wilda's
dear parents, and that through burning tears his dear
wife would have to learn to say: *Thou'rt God, when
I can't understand!"*

Ten days after she received the wire from home,
Wilda wrote:

> Friday, day of prayer, was a big help to
> me. . . . The wonderful loving Father not only
> had love for His Son, but also *had strength to
> help His Son. But He did not spare His Son.*
> What a wonderfully trustworthy Son to His
> Father our loving Lord Jesus was! Why should
> we expect Him to spare us, both in the great
> sorrow of our hearts, the unutterable longings,
> and our present situation. Oh, may we prove
> trustworthy sons!
>
> Another great help was on Hebrews 11:39.

[Someone has put it in a free paraphrase]. "They were trusted to trust without receiving what others received. They were trusted not to be offended." How I pray that I may not be offended in the least bit! He could have gotten us home in time. There is much He could have done and yet He hasn't. Oh, may my heart *truly* be able to say "not my will but thine be done."

Teach us in the silence of the Unexplained
To see Love's dearest, Love's most secret sign;
Like the White Stone, a precious thing unstained,
And as at Bethany, the glory Thine.

Arthur's comment was:

"The silence of eternity, INTERPRETED BY LOVE. . . ." We trust your love has been able to find the right interpretations. . . .

There has been plenty of quiet Bible study, and God has been speaking to our hearts to humble and enrich. . . . Last Sunday, in the little service the two of us have together, we read over the story of the Lord asleep in the boat during the storm, and saw then the faith that is at home in trouble (to the extent of reposing in the midst of the commotion in unguarded and unconcerned sleep) placed alongside the disciples' lack of faith. Their lack of faith expressed itself in rushing to the first source of tangible, visible support it could find and demanding immediate attention. The faith of the Lord was so in touch with the things not seen and eternal, *so homed in the eternal purposes of God,* that with a perfect assurance of UNWRECKABILITY of God's schedule and plan, He could sink into a care-less sleep. We often think the Lord chooses the most awkward times to sleep! But if we have our faith in stock, and available for use, then instead of rushing to Him with our reproaches, we can cry: "Sleep on,

Lord," even though the boat may be covered with waves. . . .

We are very happy here in our home. Lilah, going on two years has all she needs, and even playmates to enjoy herself with. [The Chinese children in the compound and the children of the Russian sometimes came over.] Her latest is a very tomboyish desire to climb trees. It slows up our walks with her considerably, for every tree we come to, she walks up to it, and with her arms around it, demands help in climbing. We have been entertained with the number of false alarms we have had, and have long since decided that we are quite right where we are, and will start to think otherwise only as *the boot* is actually visible. . . .

Both Wilda and Arthur found that every single green leaf put forth by them (especially in letters) was immediately challenged by the enemy of souls. Arthur had written, "Sleep on, Lord, even though the boat may be covered with waves." In less than a month a wave struck them that threatened to carry Wilda away.

For some months now Wilda had been hoping for a little brother or sister to companion Lilah. But in September, having had to lift the heavy cellar door (in one of Arthur's absences), she was stricken. Not only did she lose the little one, but she herself became so ill it looked as if she might go too. In March Arthur had feared what would become of her if he were executed. Little did he think his next fear would be that she might be taken before him. What should he do? He had no medical experience for this kind of thing. But as he prayed, God brought to mind the Roman Catholic priest who lived in Hwang-yuan. Arthur sought him out and found him very sympathetic and kind. He suggested sulfadiazine

(Arthur still had some from his Mongol clinic supplies), but he also gave some in powder form and an injection. Under the Lord's hand these did the trick, and the fever began to leave. Wilda was given back to them.

And so that storm was weathered.

It was immediately followed by testing in the realm of finances of which our next chapter will tell. But there still remained one last tremendous wave before the year 1951 closed.

Dr. C———, seeing that his medical work was in no danger of rivalry, sometimes came to the kitchen to talk with them. In December Wilda heard rumors of scarlet fever in the city, and so when the Chinese doctor returned from attending some of those cases she was not too pleased to see him come in to their little kitchen and start to play with Lilah's picture books and chat with her. After he left she tried to disinfect these as best she could (Lilah had so few toys and only three books) but two nights before Christmas, the little one would not eat her supper. She complained of a sore throat, and when they carried her up to her faraway bedroom she felt feverish. Hurriedly they got out the medical book and by the light of the candle looked for "symptoms." Just when they got to those resembling Lilah's that invaluable book said, "At this stage consult your physician." Arthur threw the book into the corner and got down on his knees. He *did* have a Great Physician. The first impression that came was to get baby out of that icebox of a bedroom. So he wrapped her up in blankets again and sent her down to the warm kitchen with her mother, while he tore up the beds and lowered them over the balcony to the ground below. Then he proceeded to set them up in the kitchen. Arthur wrote later:

Lilah's bed fits easily into Plymires' pantry.
Wilda's bed makes a nice couch in the day, and
I'm like the sick of the palsy with a movable bed
that takes the floor at the critical moment. . . .
We're busier these days. I have had to winnow
the grain, roast it, grind it, all in the last two
days. I am the *tiao-shui-tih* too (the carry water-
er) to say nothing of stoker, baker, and other
things—doctor included. I still have one step
lower and I'm anticipating that with pleasure (?),
viz. *shih-fen-tih* (collector of dung to burn for
fuel) with the fork and basket!

Wilda wrote:

On December 19 Arthur had a sleepless night
because of his tooth which has been bothering off
and on for six months. The next day he went to
have it taken out. The doctor [Dr. C.———,
not a dentist of which there was none in Hwang-
yuan] broke it off. He took all afternoon to do
that and Arthur came home shaking like a leaf;
and he had to go back the next day. This had to
be followed by a day in bed, so I had my turn
finding out how much he does for us and that "it
ain't no joke" to stoke a coal stove with brushwood continually for a time long enough to cook
breakfast and dinner in one go; and incidentally,
do all the other things which have to be done
while there's a fire. Great life! Carrying Lilah
up and down stairs didn't help me either. I developed a bad cough which has ended in a heavy
cold made worse by getting up with Lilah. For
that little lady decided not to be outdone and gave
us a sleepless night (December 23). She developed a dreadful fever on the twenty-fourth.
Praises be, we have sulfadiazine and started her
on that. She was plenty sick and now the rash
has come and strawberry tongue . . . we con-
clude she has scarlet fever. Nearly every mission-

ary family up here before us has lost a baby
from scarlet fever; we think the altitude is too
high for the strain on the little hearts. So you
can imagine our feelings! . . . The Lord is
gracious.

For Christmas cheer Wilda had previously nursed
a small rosebush in a pot, and had "snowed" it with
tiny flakes of cotton and saved a red candle to light in
front of it. But on December 25 they were fighting
for Lilah's life. Every half-hour for two nights she
would cry for a drink, kick off her bedding, toss, and
doze. *God who spared not His only Son* was the
Christmas message that rang through their hearts.
Would He ask their only begotten? But He is always
harder on Himself than on His children. The sulfa
certainly helped, and by New Year's Day we heard:
"She's a pale, droopy shadow of her normal
happy self, but she has started eating at least and
seemed to be over the fever."

Only a few days before she developed the sore
throat Arthur had written: "He would have us without care. Just so our wee lass is with us!" Then the
wee lass was stricken. It never seemed to fail. Every
testimony to God's faithfulness was followed by a test
as to whether they really believed it or not. A month
before Christmas, much tried financially, Arthur had
written a poem, "E'en There Will I Trust." Now
as he knelt beside the tossing form of his feverish
little daughter, his own words were flashed into
Arthur's mind.

> . . . though my heart quake with fear,
> E'en there will I trust. Even there.

"Five words," jeered the Devil, "now prove them!"
There are heart searchings which only Heaven
ever sees. "Satan asked to have you," said our Lord

at one time, "that he might sift you as wheat" (Luke 22:31, A.S.V.). Then He added the only words which make it possible to believe that it was a *God of Love* who gave such permission. "But *I* made supplication for thee, that thy faith fail not." Someone has said that we can be tossed in the winnowing basket and fall *until we hit that prayer* of our great Intercessor. But we fall no farther: His prayer holds us. "And do thou, when once thou hast turned again, establish thy brethren." There is the reason for permission to use the winnowing basket. Out of that sieve came I and II Peter.

And out of this sieve came the cry:

> . . . through Thy fire would I learn
> "Thou'rt God," when I can't understand.

CHAPTER SIX

The Bamboo Curtain Versus the Feather Curtain of God

U P TO SEPTEMBER, 1951, they had not been tested financially. The Mission put money in the bank at Shanghai for them and Arthur telegraphed for it as he had need of it. But in the autumn of that year Red China had ordered all funds from abroad to be frozen. Arthur and Wilda did not hear this, but Felix pounced on it with joy.

Felix (the head of the Hwangyuan police force) had lost his face because of them, through no fault of their own; and no heathen Oriental will ever forgive that. It was in the days when the Kingfisher was hoping to convert Arthur. Their belongings had been searched by the police, and Felix had helped himself to their two cameras. The Kingfisher just happened to hear about this and immediately ordered Felix to return the cameras. Both Wilda and Arthur would gladly have lost those articles rather than have this happen, for they knew immediately that Felix would revenge his loss of face in time. But the matter was not in their hands.

As we know, September days were taken up with Wilda's illness and it was not until the middle of October that Arthur awoke with a start to the realization that the bank had not yet answered his request for money. Something must be wrong? They began to economize on everything.

By this time Ben and Timothy were returned from their itinerations and once more haunted the little kitchen and the loving missionaries for fellowship. It was while Ben was in one day that Arthur involuntarily, half-thinking aloud, wondered that they would do if the remittance did not arrive soon. Within a few minutes Ben was handing them $150,-000.00 (about $7.00 U.S.). They were ashamed and taken aback but he would not listen to them. Making a covenant together that never again should Ben learn of their financial status, they accepted it as a loan, with great gratitude.

I have in my hand a tiny calendar of 1951 and on the back of the little pages are printed the messages with which God had particularly comforted them during each month.

For October, 1951, is written: *Now shalt thou see what I will do . . .* (This chapter will show how wonderfully that was fulfilled.) Underneath this is written—"Five smooth stones." From Charles Fox they had read this: "There are five stones which will bring down any giant. They are: *God is, God has, God can, God will, God does.*"

From these we see how the Bible narratives became very precious. Job's experience (they began to pray for their friends as well as for themselves): Esther's; Daniel's; Peter's, and so on. Psalm 91 had long been a special comfort.

The terror by night. Knock! Knock! at your door, late at night. Communist police, "Everybody up and out! We must search your house." That was the terror by *night,* happening all over the land.

"You have heard the accusations! What shall we do with this man?"

"Shoot him! Away with him!" the people are forced to cry. That is *the arrow that flieth by day.*

But Wilda and Arthur had noticed another verse—Psalm 91:4: *He shall cover thee with his feathers, and under his wings shalt thou trust.*

Arthur's poetical mind seized on the imagery. "Here we are, Wilda!" he had said. This is *the Feather Curtain of God.* The mother-bird's wings come down over the little chicks and they are sheltered from whatever is attacking. Cuddled up close to the mother-hen all they see are her feathers around them—and that is all we are supposed to look at! The feather-wings of God sheltering us."

It was a blessing to both of them.

October 31, 1951. Five or six days' coal supply left, fourteen days' flour and half a pound of sugar!

On the back of October the little calendar also has, "I am Now come. . . . Shout. . . . . Now, Lord, do!" Obviously lessons from Joshua 5:14: "As captain of the host of the Lord am I *now* come." Now Jericho was straitly shut up. This was their spiritual pattern; divine leadership, then faith's shout and expectancy. But what to do in actuality? The physical pattern? Well, write to Shanghai and ask the bank why money was not coming.

Begin to substitute cheaper things to save their dwindling pennies. For instance that huge stove! It had always eaten up two-thirds of their remittance in fuel. Arthur put a brick in the firebox and so made it smaller. That used less coal but still the money did not come.

The next effort was to light a fire only twice a day, morning and evening. Arthur fixed up a hay-box, and Wilda cooked their lunch in the pressure cooker while she made breakfast. Putting the cooker in the hay-box it stayed warm till noon, and with a thermos of hot water they had enough. Winter days were

sunshiny and they all wore wadded clothes. Arthur
began to look for brushwood to burn instead of coal,
and (as we have seen) contemplated making the
poor native's kind of coal ball, which is coal dust
mixed with manure.

They were down to three tattered old one-
thousand-dollar bills (equivalent to 15¢ U.S. money),
when a telegram came: "We have sent two million,
then one million. Understand this has been frozen in
Sining by police order. Without police permission no
bank will issue you your money." It was signed by
the Shanghai bank.

Oh, so this was the procedure! He must apply to
Felix for money which the Mission had already al-
located to them. So up the street to the familiar old
office goes Arthur and presents himself before Felix.

"I understand that the Sining police have frozen
our funds from Shanghai, but that I must apply to
you for them by new government regulation. I have
only this money left," producing and showing his
tattered bills. Enough to buy three match boxes that
was all, as both he and Felix knew. "What do I do
now?"

"Go back and write out your report," was the curt
answer, "and we'll investigate."

Back Arthur goes to the arduous task of writing a
report in Chinese character. But at last it is finished
and he returns to Felix's footstool, so to speak. By
him stood a scruffy little runner. This latter reached
out for the report, stuffed it into his pocket and said
casually, "All right, go home. This is our affair."

Still with only fifteen cents' worth of tattered lucre
in his pocket Arthur returned to that kitchen. It was
winter, remember. It took Felix *six weeks* "to investigate," but as Arthur has often told American

audiences since, "It did not take the Lord six weeks!"

As he entered the compound, cold and despairing, he saw the postman standing there.

"Oh, *Ma Mu-shih!*" he cried. "A million dollars has been telephoned to you from Chungking! Come up to the office tonight and get it!"

The Feather Curtain of God had softly fallen over His children as man deliberately planned starvation for them. They called it *The Miracle Million* (worth about $45.00 U.S.), for it was truly that. Mr. Ellison (C.I.M. workers in Chungking) hearing of their plight had taken a million dollars to the telephone office in Chungking. "Here you are! Please send this to *Ma Liang-chen Mu-shih,* Hwangyuan, Tsinghai" (Arthur's Chinese name and address). The telephone was the only route left that was not frozen. Moreover, Mr. Ellison had applied for exit, and two days later his permit came through and he had to leave. He knew nothing of the "only-fifteen-cents-left condition of the Mathews' family on that day! "Now shalt thou see what I will *do,*" our Father-Mother-God had said, and softly down upon His little children descended the Feather-Wing-Curtain. If the money had been sent *by any other route,* it would have been intercepted by Felix!

Arthur took no chances. First of all he repaid Ben the $150,000.00, then bought coal, potatoes, flour, everything they would need. He tried to transmute the money into food and things the police could not touch. And this was the reason there was heat in the kitchen when Lilah-girlie came down with scarlet fever. Arthur writes:

> Things swept gaily around the bend a week before Christmas for us, when an old Chungking cobber[1] came to light with one million . . . we

---

[1] Australian expression for chum.

cannot yet fathom how it managed to run the blockade, enough that we have a heavenly Father who makes the schedule. Into that schedule came one of my offending molars that needed a spot of do-re-mi[2] in my pocket to persuade me to take the plunge with a local doctor of dismal repute. Having lost a big piece of it six months ago I have been able to keep it reasonably quiet till the very night the million arrived—and then *on that night* could not the person concerned sleep! I hurried round next morning to get as much tummy-fodder packed away as possible, then off I went, goofy enough to believe that one tug would do it. Boy, oh, boy! Two hours on a backless bench on a freezing cold dirt floor providing valuable experience for what seemed to be a hopeless case, and then another next day . . . and I still have half a tooth for a home dentist to tackle!

We sang Hallelujah the day the million came, I can tell you. This reminds me to thank you for your kind offer of help, but as luck would have it *there is a great gulf fixed between us;* things cannot come from your end. The trouble is the efficient model refrigerator that . . . seals up what we get . . . before it can reach us.

He had to be very careful what he said for his letters were often opened at the Chinese post office and read by those who knew some English before being forwarded. He later referred to frozen funds as *lucre on ice.*

As the C.I.M. learned of Felix' intention to starve the Mathews' family others began to plan ways of help, and prayer went up in a great volume. One missionary found that a ten-thousand-dollar bill (45¢ in U.S.) would just fit an unimportant Chinese envelope, and once a week sent them such. This just paid for Lilah's milk supply. Chinese do not milk

---

[2] Arthur's pun on the slang "dough" for money.

cows, but Moslems do and Tibetans milk the yak. An old Tibetan woman was accustomed to bringing them two bowls each day, and this was kept for Lilah. Of course the lack of milk affected the teeth of both Wilda and Arthur, and Arthur's toothache became more painful. But where was the money to get it pulled?

On the back of the month of December the little calendar holds this: CAST FOUR ANCHORS AND PRAYED FOR DAY. This was obviously a reference to Acts 27:27-29 (A.S.V.) : . . . *as we were driven to and fro in the sea of Adria . . . they let go four anchors from the stern and prayed for day.*

These "four anchors" they found in Andrew Murray's formula for trial.

1. Say, He brought me here. It is by His will I am in this strait place and in that fact I will rest.
2. He will keep me here in His love and give me grace to behave as His child.
3. Then He will make the trial a blessing, teaching me the lessons He intends for me to learn.
4. In His good time He can bring me out again— how and when He knows. So let me say, I am (1) here by God's appointment; (2) in His keeping; (3) under His training; (4) for His time.

So, by faith, Wilda and Arthur Mathews cast these four anchors. The first sign that these anchors would hold came in the early arrival of a Christmas parcel! It was from the McIntoshes at Sining and was followed in two weeks by a second one. Wilda writes:

Amy had said it was a tin of cookies so we weren't prepared for the large carton box containing not only a large 5 lb. tin of several kinds of cookies but also another small tin of cookies, a large fruit cake, sugar, tea, a cocoa tin of hard candy and two packages of candles, raisins, lard, and marmalade. Among the cookies were some in animal shapes for Lilah. How her eyes sparkled as she saw the doggies! It was the first candy she had had. You just can't imagine what it did mean to us. We haven't had a dessert or any kind of sweet thing for so long that we feel starved for it.

This took care of their "tummies," but what of fuel, dentist charges, and other necessities?

Arthur remembers walking up and down in the little icy-cold bedroom singing and praying, "Master, the tempest is raging, the billows are tossing high . . . carest Thou not that we perish?"

It seemed to come like an answer: "It is not the storm that worries the Lord Jesus. It is the *unbelief of the disciples.*"

Six weeks from the time they had notified Felix that all they had left was three thousand (15¢), a policeman arrived in their courtyard. He came into the kitchen, sat down, looked up at the ceiling and said, "Well, how are you getting on?"

"I told you forty-two days ago that we had only three thousand (15¢) left," answered Arthur. "You know that your government has frozen our money and that we cannot get it unless you give it to us. I have tried again and again to contact our bank in Shanghai but there has been no response." At that moment Arthur truly had none of it *in cash* left. After inspecting the ceiling for a few moments longer, the policeman got up and left. Now note this: He had come in by the gate, but he did not return that way. Some idea had come into his head *to go through the chapel* and out of the compound that way. As he entered the chapel, a mailboy from the post office came in by the gate. And before the policeman had reached the street, he was saying to Arthur: "Here is a registered letter for you." It was from the bank and contained one million dollars ($45.00 U.S.). If the postman had come a minute earlier, Arthur would have had to confess the possession of this money. But God's Feather Curtain had fallen.

The bamboo curtain shouts and bellows as it descends, boasts and preens itself.

The Feather Curtain of God falls silently. It is soft and cuddly to the sheltered one; but intangible, mysterious and baffling to the outsider.

Felix, on hearing his policeman's report of their destitution, sent word they might draw whatever amounts he cared to give in response to their estimate of monthly needs. But there must be a fresh application each month. This performance was described by an onlooker as the monthly belly-crawl.

Another answer to prayer at this time was for Lilah's scarlet fever aftermath. Bob Ament (another C.I.M.-er) had the happy thought to send vitamin pills. Arthur writes to thank him:

March 12, 1952. Your second installment of pills safely arrived the day before yesterday. The first parcel had been looked at and seeing it only had forty odd in it, I jumped to the conclusion that some had been filched, but with the second parcel in, our fears are relieved. Lilah took two on successive days and on the second evening we were amazed to hear her call for her supper an hour before it was due and keep it up. Five minutes after she had been set down she was waving an empty bowl in one hand and spoon in the other and calling all and sundry to witness. Then we had to fill her bowl with our food, and when that was done great hunks of dry bread were stuffed into her mouth. It was quite exciting for a change —usually she sits for half an hour till we'd get fed up with talking to her and then we'd have to stuff what we could into her and she'd return with an obliging vomit and bring it all back again!

Another snowfall last night and bright sun today, so everywhere is sloppy. I put Lilah on an old bench and push her up and down to give her a taste of sledding, but we daren't let her play in it because she'd have no shoes to change into. . . . It's a great game paddling down to the creek these days—I go early before it gets too slushy, and take off socks, just wear my prehistorics; even so, plenty of cold ice, snow, and slush slops in. I've a new look on life now. I'm constantly thinking of the hungry-tummied beggars since our December experience . . . and when it's sloppy like this my sympathies are with the poor water-carrying women with their cloth shoes. . . .

We certainly are learning that the man who really lives does *not live by bread alone* (even though we do think a steak and kidney pie . . . very nice!). These often do, but *should* have nothing to do with the walk of faith. When they do, then we end in Egypt like Abraham. . . . In our Lord's temptation the point was to crack Him along the line of complete, willing submission to the appointment of place, circumstances, and methods of God's will . . . which, coming down to our level, means that for us . . . to deny ourselves that complete submission and sheer trust, is to deny our spirits the sustenance they require, and will reduce us to living by bread alone— which is not living but starvation.

It was during this time of being "driven up and down in Adria" that the Lord gave Arthur this green leaf out of the drought of financial stress and sickness.

In Adria's tempest-tossed wastes,
My barque through the dark deeps is driv'n;
The canvas all torn from my masts,
My timbers by stormy waves riv'n.
Yet there faith's assurance rings clear,
E'en there will I trust, *EVEN THERE.*

All hope for deliverance had gone,
Despair's chilly gloom shrouded all;
No sun's ray through threat'ning cloud shone
To brighten the future's dark pall.
Yet there though my heart quake with fear,
E'en there will I trust, *EVEN THERE.*

My brook's daily waters had dried,
All replenishing springs scorched bare;
Resourceless in sore need I cried
To a God who seemed not to care.
Though trembling, triumphant I bow
E'en now I will trust, *EVEN NOW.*

The barrel of meal empties fast,
The tempter crowds close with his lies;
"Can God?" Ah! He's failed you at last,
"In wilderness find fresh supplies."
Perish doubts! Though I know not how,
E'en now will I trust, *EVEN NOW.*

'Tis the way of the cross I own,
And it leads through the gloom to gold,
"A corn of wheat" in dust I'm sown,
Self's vain showy husk there must mold,
Though entombed in dust I can grow,
E'en so will I trust, *EVEN SO.*

CHAPTER SEVEN

The Monthly Belly-Crawl

A T FIRST I THOUGHT that this inelegant epithet had popped up out of Major Arthur Mathews' soldier past; but I am told, not so. It was coined by a fellow-sufferer as the only truly descriptive name for the humiliating experience the missionary was forced to go through every time he needed to ask for some of his own money. Please remember that the sum of three million Chinese dollars ($135.00 U.S.), which the bank had sent for the Mathews' family and Felix refused to give up, was part of their salary from the C.I.M. As said before, their letters home were censored by the Chinese, and it was necessary to use expressions that would convey information beyond what such a censor would understand. And the most constant plea for prayer through all the letters of this particular year was, "Please remember the monthly belly-crawl." With apology to our readers for its crudeness, we are deliberately retaining the term in order that its very roughness may shake us awake— us who consider ourselves too dainty for what may some day descend upon us also, though we pray God to spare us and our country.

To begin with, there was never any time of day nor night when Arthur could be sure they would condescend to receive him. Each month he had to write out in detail an estimate of what they would need to spend for fuel, clothes, and food, etc. They always figured that, without luxuries, one million

($45.00 U.S.) a month was needed for the three of them, because the coal alone cost two-thirds of that. Felix never once allowed Arthur that much, and gradually he began to diminish what he did condescend to grant.

But as the middle of each month drew near, Arthur would make out his estimate slip and proceed to the police station. Sometimes he would go early to see if he could get any inkling as to what time the officials would be likely to see him. It was the sentry at the door who held him up first. Although everyone in the small town had heard of the white man's predicament and knew why he must present himself at the police station, the police themselves pretended to be in perpetual ignorance of the reason.

"What ya doin' here?" the sentry might shout.

"I want to submit my estimate sheet for the police's ratification," Arthur would humbly answer.

"He hasn't time now! Come back again," might be the rejoinder. Sometimes the sentry would simply grab the estimate sheet and stuff it in his own pocket. That was perhaps the worst of all. A nearly bare cupboard was frequently behind Arthur, or an empty coalbin in winter.

More often than not he was told to wait. Outside in all kinds of weather, snow, slush, rain as well as sunny skies he had to hang around the entrance hour after hour, with the native passers-by staring at him. To laugh at the foreigner stood you in good stead with the government so there were those who would like to make fun of him. All this he must endure and at the end of the day be told to come back again.

The second day when he arrived he was told the official was sick—he must wait until after the week end. On Monday he went back, waited for hours and no one paid any attention. Went home for a meal and came back. At length the sentry had a message for him. "We've got to do some more investigating— wait until we contact you."

When at length an amount was granted, the slip stamped and given to him, Arthur took it to the bank and was handed the amount written down. There was never any trouble at the bank. It is of slight interest to tell that the Chinese bank had on its walls huge pictures of Russian officers completely encircling it—and not one Chinese face among them. But glimpses through the letters may help us to see the situation.

March 9, 1952. Pray for Roberta's hubby. [Clarence Preedy in Sining whose name must be disguised in letters. Most often he is "Seepy" for C. P.] We wait for later news and have cake and cookies ready to send if he is not on compulsory bread and water [i.e., prison], having been blessed ourselves with timely help. We thought Mother Hubbard was getting down on her uppers and took early precautions (*a scrap of paper and a short walk every few days* to back it up)[1] and now for some reason our lucre turns up.

March 15, 1952. We have enough for a little while and I bought flour yesterday, but pray ahead of things in case we land in another Zarephath. I said to Wilda last night, "Doesn't the Lord know we are not Hudson Taylor?" Spring is our hardest time; no potatoes, carrots, etc., till the new crop comes in . . . it is no use thinking about it though; we'd go bats if we did. It seems logical to think that a faith mission would be tested along the line of what is reputedly its strong point—viz., faith. My conclusion is that some of us must have had a pretty sickly kind of faith to require all this toughening

---

[1] Covered words meaning his estimate application and walk to the police station.

March 31, 1952. . . . morale has had another
boost with your circular of the seventeenth just
in. . . . Our mail is always ahead of Seepy's so
I'll post to him this afternoon and enclose yours
and a home letter or two. He had a week to wait
before the time due to make his monthly b——
-crawl and was about out of bread. Our cake and
cookies arrived in time not only to help his batch-
ing but also his starvation end-of-the-month diet.

We had a heart-warmer yesterday—a package
with a pair of shoes . . . odds and ends of dresses,
petticoats that can be made over for Lilah.

This was slipped to them by the Russian Christian
who had *bought* the shoes from Arthur the previous
year and been given other things by Wilda. Arthur
continues:

Incidentally, the shoes were originally Row-
land's! The boots I have are rotten underneath
and part along the edges, and were all I had until
yesterday (except for my knee-length felt boots)
so if we are not able to pick up our things at
Lanchow, on the way out, I'll have something not
quite prehistoric!

April 6, 1952. Seepy's humble co-operators are
in full swing. His "little member" puts him in
Nehemiah's book (6:6 d) with a Gashmu at his
heels. Guess he needs prayer badly, and when it
comes our turn add, "Amen!" Yesterday I received a slip from the bank . . . released through
my energetic representation. Haven't been able to
verify. Have to have a chop on it, and so far
drawn a blank. Moved upstairs today, so have
more pleasant scenery and smells. If they're
releasing dough for us here, they can't be expecting us to move in a hurry. So we are getting pots
out ready to plant lettuce seedlings and beetroot—
with two-year-old seeds!

April 15, 1952. Evidently my success in getting lucre has met with favor to the extent that now mousie's little tracks all have traps set in them. . . . R. M. C. arrived—no dough since the end of January, and like Pharaoh's second batch of kine.

R.M.C. is Dr. Rupert M. Clarke. He was originally at Hwalung station, but when his money ran out, he was left three days without food and then sent to Clarence Preedy at Sining, and Preedy was told to support him! But we were all glad the two men were together. Arthur continues:

Funny how we plan everything so carefully and then God walks sovereignly right across the lot with something far better. Our "leaf" should not wither for we are His "planting." And planting includes a lot of preparation of site with a view to constant supply of water. It means selection of the tree, its type, its maturity, etc. Our planting beside these waters means that for our leaf to wither there must be a denial by us of *supply sources*. May that never be true of us.

May 28, 1952. Wilda needs to go soon to the dentist but local stinginess means that we have to walk wary. The three of us get only three-quarters of what the two of them get [Dr. Clarke and Mr. Preedy] and we are in a pretty expensive spot. Next b—— -crawl the snake won't be in it! I'll plead Wilda's health and so on. The estimate list of necessities grows; Lilah needs shoes, Wilda dentistry, I need a shirt or two.

July 18, 1952. My b—— -crawl last Monday and Tuesday (after five very worm-like presentations!) only produced seven hundred thousand ($31.50 U.S.). Teeth extractions are jam in comparison to sucking blood out of stones. One more in the middle of next month and we'll be running into shoals. Pray hard for guidance. If the Lord wants to use our shoals as a means of moving,

then we're happy enough to run aground; but
we don't want to be presumptuous and try stunt
flying.

This is a reference to their guess as to Red policy.
From the treatment of Dr. Clarke they concluded that
the Regime would not give them their exit permits
as long as they had any money left. This proved to
be true.

> September 10, 1952. I could get quite a sink-
> ing feeling if I stopped to think of next week end
> [when his September b——— -crawl was due] but
> the Lord was so good last time . . . all I had to
> do was to get to the bottom of the ladder and say
> my piece . . . many are praying and "greasing
> the runaways."

But after the September application for funds
Arthur writes:

> We can surely feel for Moses during the pre-
> liminaries to the Exodus. I've every sympathy for
> his parting fling at the end (Exod. 11:8 . . . *and
> he went out from Pharoah in hot anger*). I was
> numbering up my crawls, and as far as I can see,
> I beat Moses hollow!
>
> The plagues must have seemed a painfully slow
> way of staging deliverance, but if Israel (with all
> they saw of God's wonders) could descend to
> such depths of failure, what would they have been
> like if the process of revaluation of the might of
> God had been simplified or shortened! So it must
> be with us.
>
> Our current skirmish opened on Monday the
> 15th and closed on Saturday the 20th. By the
> time it was over, I was shaking almost as badly
> as I was after two and a half hours in the dentist's
> bench last December. First off, I was sent home;
> next day told to return two days later; then the

following morning I sat outside in the dirt persistently refusing suggestions to buzz off, till at last when I was beginning to weaken, the required came to hand and I was able to empty the till. [This was their last bit of money in the local bank.] Not a very wonderful reward for all the humble pie I had had to eat. Our guess, and yours too no doubt, is that we are popular enough to be kept till the Mathews' household is really hungry.

The worst part of these experiences (which were plentifully sprinkled with Chinese curses—and the latter are filthy, foul epithets, not just blasphemy) was the suspense and tension. Hanging around the doorstep like a beggar in all sorts of weather was bad enough. To do that for hours, and then go home empty-handed, wondering if you slipped up in wisdom somewhere, that got on the nerves.

But God was teaching His children as He taught His own Son—*made perfect through suffering*—and who learned how to become the Lamb that opened not His mouth as He was led to the slaughter. In this same letter Arthur writes:

John says, I FOUND *myself in the isle which is called Patmos*—not one jot of credit does he give to the might and organization of Nero's Rome. And not one mention escapes him of the scourging, accusations, etc., that he must have endured before eventually "finding" himself there.

He was "found" there just as Philip was "found" at Azotus, and the Mathews' family are "found" here. The means, circumstances, decisions that led to his finding himself there are unimportant, mere things of time. Faith discerns even behind the Beast the hand of God—for second causes make good disguises and baffle any eye but the eye of faith. So to enlarge on the why and the wherefore; to blame himself or his

charges; to weigh past decisions for or against;
(I guess you've heard little else over the past) is
not on John's mind; nor does he allow any imag-
inings, criticisms, wishful sighings to occupy his
thoughts. A more ideal field for just such thoughts
could hardly be found. So there is a great deal
of comfort for us in John's early verses of the
Revelation.

Patmos does not spell an unjust God, an un-
caring God; nor does it spell the overthrow of
God's plans. Patmos is where He, who was given
the tongue of the LEARNER (disciple, Isa. 50:4,
marg.) that He should *know how to speak a word
to sustain him that is weary* (marg.), speaks clear-
est the words that weary souls need to sustain
them *in the . . . patience of Jesus Christ.*

We have tried to obey the Patmos command to
"write what thou seest" though the flesh has often
complained, and the spirit too.

In November Wilda writes:

We don't have any more "beans" [money] than
last month but we do still have some vegetables,
fuel, and flour; not much, but what a difference
between a little and nothing."

From Arthur came a letter that was torn and
words missing, showing it had been mutilated by the
censor. Discernible are:

Wilda . . . to visit longer. Money still tighter
than ever. Have made four visits and drawn
blanks. Pray, *Pray.* PRAY!

Paul Gerhardt has become a new friend. I
keep going over and over some of his verses,
and today's is:

> Although to make God falter,
> The powers of hell combine;
> One jot they cannot alter

Of His all-wise design.
All Projects and volition
Of His eternal mind;
Despite all opposition,
Their due fulfillment find.
All faithless murmurs leaving,
Bid them a last Good-night;
No more thy vexed soul grieving,
Because things seem not right;
Wisely His scepter wielding,
God sits in regal state,
No power to mortals yielding,
Events to regulate.

Arthur ends with this meditation.

The Lord sometimes has to show us, not only the power of the one against us, but *also the weakness of our own hearts.* His battles are not won through strength and prowess, but through weakness thoroughly weakened, that refuses to do anything at all for itself but *trust* in His faithfulness—even when to trust seems folly.

Part Two

THE BURSTING OF THE GREEN

CHAPTER EIGHT

The Best Wine . . . Now

WITH THE BEGINNING of the second year (1952) came the Accusation Meetings of the Communist Regime. These struck Clarence Preedy in Sining first and on January 18 Arthur writes:

> The meetings are in full spate now and our neighbor has sent out a wire, *"Pray"* . . . Thank God for the . . . praying folk and others. It's a big bit of prayer discipline for them, too. . . . God is using us to teach you loved ones things you'd never have appreciated without it . . .
>
> My thought for the prayer helpers is from Genesis 18:22: *Abraham stood yet before the Lord,* and Abraham's words, *I have taken upon me.* . . . It implies something *upon me.* I have a responsibility upon me and I *stand yet* until God lifts it.

By spring, 1952, they had seen more than six hundred [1] members of the China Inland Mission Family escape to safety—not to speak of the children. This left only thirty-four others, conspicuous among whom were the five in the Northwest because they were the farthest away. As prayer in the homelands began to focus on them we want you to watch what God did.

At first it was difficult to see those hundreds of their fellows pouring over the border into safety and

---

[1] This number includes 36 who were in Hong Kong just before the official withdrawal order was given in January, 1951.

to be left behind. They naturally wondered—was something wrong with them? Were they failing to do something they should be doing?

About this time a tract on Throne Life came into their hands in which the writer stated that Christians *have access to the King,* and as such they have the privilege of presenting and pressing their claims. Instances were given where even missionaries, frustrated continually along certain lines, took their stand in prayer that they had *Throne Rights* over that situation and in His name commanded victory. It is the Christians' privilege to press their Throne Rights, said the writer, as those who are seated together with Christ in the heavenlies. This phase of truth troubled Arthur and Wilda Mathews. Had they failed in spiritual warfare to command the situation?

For several months after reading that, they sought to do it. They pressed their claims for deliverance upon God. He had promised it. "The prey of the terrible SHALL BE DELIVERED." *"Now,* O Lord, perform it," they cried. But this "claiming" only wore them out and made them restless. The gate remained barred as tight as ever.

Wilda wrote her sister:

> . . . in John 11:40 if we believe we *will* see the glory of God. Believe to the uttermost, not that He could have, but that He *really is* going to perform the miracle. Every day we wonder, and every new week we hope it may be His time.

Here we see faith straining forward. Daily they watched the calendar and ticked off the days, and though there were moments of victory there was a great deal of restlessness.

April 18 was Easter in 1952 and as it drew near, Wilda determined that it was not going to be another black day. She set herself to study the resurrection story and the resurrection life. As she came to the part that Peter played in the courtyard of the high priest's palace she suddenly felt heart-condemned. She had not said, *I know Him not* but she had no *joy*. She was not bitter, but she *was* frustrated and restless. Her opportunity to witness to the Chinese eyes around them that she *did* know the Lord and that He was satisfying her drought—had she shown that? If not, wasn't that *denying the Lord* before man? On her knees before Him she confessed it as such, and the result was *a glorious Easter*.

But it was yet some two months before God perfected the experience by giving it to Arthur also. It began without notice that a spiritual crisis had arrived. In fact, the scene was a very commonplace one for those days. They were both up on the balcony enjoying the June weather. This little upper veranda was a joy we have not mentioned. Its view lifted them above the city's drabness and dirt. A hill was on each side of the narrow Hwangyuan valley which lay before them, and beyond the gap where the hills approached each other could be seen the jagged serrated peaks of a far mountain range. The sun sank behind the right-hand hill, and the glory of his setting lit up crag and rock, and threw streamers of color across the sky.

Lilah was in bed and turning over for the night's sleep.

Wilda was mending clothes—a daily task now. Arthur's shirt tails had to be cut off and used to patch shoulder holes. Lilah's winter clothes were all too short now and extensions had to be found and made.

Arthur was sitting by, thumbing through a Weymouth's translation when he came to Ephesians 5:10:

and learn in your own experiences what is fully pleasing to the Lord. He looked up.

"Wilda, listen to this," and he read it to her. "What do you think, dear, is well-pleasing to the Lord in these our experiences?" It was a chance to tell of her own private Easter message. Not to receive it joyfully was to deny the Lord before men. They talked it back and forth, and later during the next day or two also. As they ruminated light poured in. A few nights later it came to Arthur like a flash: the Son had left Heaven, not *submitting* to the will of God, but *delighting*. Up to now they had been submitting; rather feverishly submitting because they felt they should press His promises. "Lord, why do You delay? We could be out spear-heading advance into new mission fields! Open the door *now,* Lord!"

They had been acting like servants who don't want to do it but have to, because they can't get out of it. What a different attitude was the Son's! There came a day in June when together Arthur and Wilda knelt before the Lord and abandoned themselves to live on in that stinted little kitchen as long as He wished them to. And the peace of God poured in like a flood bringing such joy as they had not known before. But we will let Arthur tell it, as he wrote it for the prayer friends at home.

> June 27, 1952. There are many things to tell of the Lord's wondrous doings for us. But in all the stirrings of inside thoughts the one that wants to jump out first is: THOU HAST KEPT THE BEST WINE TILL NOW.
>
> It may seem strange to you, but it is true! And true of the two of us. . . . For some time we felt that we had been getting nowhere; wherever we looked there was the taunting mirage of when will

we exit? . . . We searched our hearts and our motives; we had thought that our prayers were what the Lord would have them; but still the feeling persisted. [Then he told of their experience on the balcony.]

Just to say submission to the will of God did not seem to go deep enough, for we had been trying for a long time to do just that. If you had a servant you would expect submission from him, just as you would from an old bullock with a yoke on its neck. But as *sons* surely there was something more than that.

Thus we chewed and ruminated over these thoughts for a day or two, and then somehow I had my thoughts turned to Philippians 2:13 *for it is God himself whose power creates within you both the* DESIRE *and the* POWER *to execute His will* (Weymouth). That opened a door for us. Why should we go on wondering what God would have us learn when His Word told us that He had put the DESIRE into our hearts, *with the* POWER.

That we had not perceived His will meant that the DESIRE was buried under cover of something earthy—or some lesser selfish things. God's finger pointed, *In this thing ye believed not the Lord your God.* So as we uncovered the earth we could see that our prayers had selfishly centered around the shortening of the days. . . . There was none of the recklessness of faith such as the three friends of Daniel showed. Nor was there the spirit of joyous abandonment which the widow displayed in giving her two mites.

So we came to see that God wanted us to *will* with Him to stay put; not to desire to run away as quickly as we could force Him or persuade Him to let us. . . . It was natural that we should go from there to cry with David, *I* DELIGHT *to do thy will, O my God* (Ps. 40:8).

The great chords that sounded through our hearts as we touched the JOYOUSLY ABANDONED keys were really thrilling. . . .

So we are no longer stupid bullocks being driven or dragged unwillingly along a distasteful road; but sons, co-operating with all our powers, launching out wholeheartedly hand-in-hand with our Father. . . .

To express the thoughts in our hearts I had adapted lines of Bishop Ken's thus:

> Delight to *will* God's will, and you will find
> Your enemies as friends, beside you lined.

Here we see the bursting of the green. Up to now, with all the drought and parched ground, the little trees have sent out a green leaf or two, to show that life was not quenched. But as happens when the sap has full unhindered course to run throughout trunk and branches, there comes a day when all over the tree, green buds are sprouting, bursting forth. Such a sight is a thing of beauty that halts the passer-by and brings him to mute worship. *The Lord shall satisfy thy soul in drought* (Isa. 58:11) had been fulfilled.

The message above all others which the Chinese church needed was *to see that truth* lived out under circumstances equally harrowing with their own.

Wilda and Arthur had longed to serve Him; but human-like they had put their own interpretation on what service is. They thought it meant preaching with their lips. Amy Carmichael once replied to a Tamil Christian who took this meaning of service: "God didn't make you *all mouth.*" The most potent way to preach is *by life,* by living it. This was the service which the Mathews' family were to render to Him.

The immature reader may be saying, "Oh, now

they have reached the peak of spiritual surrender, God will swing open the doors and let them depart." Not so. God had more than the perfecting of Arthur and Wilda in mind. And so He will *allow the drought to increase* to the point where human rejoicing (by human will power or an extraeffervescent natural disposition) will be absolutely impossible. *Now wilt thou see what I shall do* is His Word.

"In the day the drought consumed me," cried poor Jacob. God will allow the drought to reach the consuming stage, and still the trees will be bursting with green. For this victory, severely tested, stood. They do not say they were never overcome. "Your spirit is willing, but human nature is weak," in Phillip's paraphrase of Mark 14:38: But though the human side quailed occasionally, the spirit never faltered and *never lost the peace* which came with joyous abandonment to the will of God.

Andrew Murray has said, "Faith may accept; only long-suffering inherits the promise."

Psychologically it rings true also. To again quote Andrew Murray: "In commerce, in study, in war it is so often said: *there is no safety but in advance.* . . . To stand still is to go back. To cease effort is to lose ground. To slacken the pace, before the goal is reached, is to lose the race."

These missionaries saw this truth clearly. Arthur writes:

It would be so easy to slip into the sin that all prisoners-of-war know something about, viz., the sin of allowing the circumstances to paralyze our hearts, minds, and wills so that we settle into an attitude of life that believes there is no good in doing anything. . . .

. . . the recent floods of joy. . . . I don't think it necessary for me to say that we shunned any exaggeration. Others may think so, but you [prayer helpers] and those who have been "partners in the other boat" will know how wonderfully God has revealed Himself to one and another of the Remnant. It is really true that *the best wine* has been kept until now and it comes too, just at the hiatus in our experiences, when we are doing what we ought not to have been doing—viz., "feeling the strain." The yoke is LIGHT only as it is TAKEN, and not as it is *suffered*.

And so they entered the second drought-consuming experience with "the best wine" held to their lips, and their Master's tender voice saying, "Drink, yea, *drink abundantly,* O beloved." Even so shall thy leaf be green when the heat cometh.

CHAPTER NINE

Though the Mountains Shake . . .
There Is a River

THE FIRST SIGN that a new "heat wave" was advancing on them came in the spring of 1952 when the Accusation Meetings began. Every single Chinese was forced to "criticize" himself and his neighbor in order to prove his loyalty to Communism —especially anyone who had had any connection with a foreigner. The Red Regime will not allow the belief that there can be *any* good American or Englishman. If you say so you are revealing the fact that you are pro-imperialist in your heart. You must accuse the foreigner of your acquaintance with some sin against the government in order to clear your own skirts of the suspicion that you are pro-imperialist. And to be pro-imperialist means death.

To warn one another of these things in letters required very covered speech and so we find Arthur writing:

It is encouraging that you do not mind wading into our crossword puzzles. Mary sent a good one this morning: *addled eggs going pop.* I guess ours are practically exploded by now but the effluvium hasn't got this far yet.

This refers to the accusations against Mary Guinness and her husband in Nanking city, and Arthur's surmise that unknown accusations against them were already on paper but had not yet reached Hwang-yuan. He continues:

> We have not heard from Seepy for quite awhile, and he has not been getting ours [letters] so guess that the new arrival there, plus addling eggs and their explosions, have upset the normal scheme of things. . . . The last from Seepy sometime ago mentions getting a pair of shoes for Rupert. None of the shoe-makers would believe that anyone less that an elephant could have such feet, but eventually he got someone to believe him, and the shoes were made to the required scale. Of course it would have settled matters if the elephant could have gone along to prove things, but that was out of the question! [Dr. Rupert Clarke was under house arrest.]

May 5, 1952, is marked as the day when Ben returned from Sining where he had been summoned to "confess his faults." As he went, Wilda and Arthur were much in prayer, for they knew he would be forced to criticize them in some way or other or imperil his own life. As they prayed, God gave them Psalm 138:7, 8: *Though I walk in the midst of trouble, thou wilt revive me: Thou wilt stretch forth thine hand against the wealth of mine enemies, and thy right hand will save me. Jehovah will perfect that which concerneth me.*

Both Ben and Timothy had been in the habit of dropping in each evening for fellowship, and it had greatly sweetened their days. As Ben returned from Sining he passed them by without a speech but a significant look set their hearts at rest. That evening after dark he came to them secretly and told all that had happened. He had been so helped in selecting criticisms of them that there was no new tangible thing for the Regime to lay hold of. God *had* "stretched forth his hand."

The next week Timothy was called up. Perhaps it was the easy victory in Ben's case, but there was not so much prayer made for Timothy. And when he returned some days later they knew in a second that the outcome had been unfavorable. His face was dark as he entered the compound and a cloud seemed to descend over everyone within the same walls. Gradually they learned that Timothy had played traitor not only to them but to the Chinese Christians, Pastors Jen and Chin, and so on. One must remember that Timothy had been careless originally in coming to Hwangyuan not to register with the police on arrival. This may have been used to pressure him, poor fellow. But these two boys are a very fair representation of what happened to the Chinese church as a whole when it went through the Accusation Meetings.

Timothy was now sent back to their compound to live in their midst and spy on everybody's actions. He was followed very shortly by a visit from the police who denounced them fiercely and forbade anyone in the compound to speak to the imperialists on pain of going to prison. Timothy was there to tell if it occurred.

May 14 has a sad little note:

> From then on, no one on the compound or any Christians would speak to us, or notice us in the slightest.

There were two Chinese families and themselves living in the inner courtyard; and the two pastors' families in the outer courtyard. They passed by each other daily in the common tasks of hauling water and tending their garden plots, but now it was in silence and with averted face.

More than that, the police placed the white people under arrest—they were not allowed to go outside their compound. At that Pastor Jen spoke up in alarm: "Well, sir, who is to draw their water from the river for them? And buy their food?"

The police hesitated. "He may go to the river for water and to the market for shopping but no more than that."

Life had been proscribed before, but now it would be much worse. "And shall not be careful in the year of drought [restraint]" (Jer. 17:8, A.S.V., marg.). They were to prove this. Lilah, of course, was included and she had to have more than one spanking, poor child, before she learned that she might not show her picture book to Ben, or speak to anyone.

> May 13, 1952. I'm plucking up courage to try another butcher tomorrow to have another tooth extraction. I've two to be done so I'll give him the easy one first to see how he shapes. The former butcher is on a bread-and-with-it diet.

This refers to Dr. C——. He had the misfortune to have a patient die, and the Accusation Meetings made the most of it. He was in prison for awhile, as Arthur indicates, and then he was sentenced to fifteen years of hard labor. He must be still breaking roads somewhere in China! This removed him from the master bedroom over the kitchen, but Timothy immediately moved in there! It was an excellent place for a spy besides being warm and comfortable. He could hear almost everything that went on in the kitchen below, and the front window faced the gate and garden so that he saw all who came in and everything that happened.

May 28, 1952 Arthur writes:

> One of Religious Liberty's pals [Eric Liberty]
> paid a visit to Seepy's joint [Sining] and spilled a
> bib-full of high exps. gas, so we're in the same
> boat with Seepy. [House-confined.] Ever read
> *Three Men in a Boat?* Great stuff; it may end
> that way. Pray though for Wilda and the nip if it
> does. I had my tooth stumps painlessly extracted
> a fortnight ago. [A Chinese dentist with proper
> instruments had arrived in town, he being the
> second butcher.] What a relief! I was having
> continual pain in my head, and it was that that
> persuaded me to go have another shot. The
> stumps are out with no butchering, as last time,
> and the head is O.K. . . . if I keep it up I'll be
> toothless before I get out!

The hot weather was now approaching and un-
clean conditions beneath their bedroom were a trial.
Dr. C—— had kept some Tibetan patients there, and
as these never bathe and have no idea of sanitation,
the place became smelly, dirty, and what Arthur
described as a "flea factory." Added to this the
Chinese had tied up their dog to the front window.
The communists organized a Clean-Up Movement,
part of which is to kill rats, flies, and *dogs*. Any dog
on the street is pounced upon and dispatched. Someone had written of being kept awake at night by dogs
yapping and said they were dog-tired. Arthur replies:

> Your puppy-dog tale could be matched with
> plenty of puppy dog tails from our end. Sticks
> and stones and the city braves were all alerted
> for a round up, so now our moon rides the skies
> unserenaded. I boldly (and perhaps out of turn)
> suggested to the church that the dog here should
> be released to sally forth to meet them and his
> doggy heaven, then they wouldn't have the ex-

pense of feeding him. Either the penny didn't drop or they weren't biting. I didn't say (although I felt weak enough to want to) that that would be a far lesser cruelty than half-starving the poor beast and leaving him tied up night and day in the dark corner under our bedroom windows, literally ankle-deep in filth! With the dog under our bedroom and an open toilet ten to fifteen yards from the kitchen door, can you wonder that, in spite of all our precautions, Lilah had an attack of dysentery?

This attack came just about ten days after their experience of the joy of abandonment. Every testimony of victory was immediately challenged—it never failed.

Dysentery is one of the most formidable baby diseases that white children face in the Orient. Many, many have died from it, and they often go *so quickly*. Little Lilah had the bloody flux type and soon she was screaming with pain. For half an hour she just sat in her little rocker, rocking back and forth and screaming—she wouldn't allow her mother to touch her. Arthur went on the street to find suitable medicine but could get nothing. He came back and got down on his knees and prayed.

This was the period when letters between Sining and Hwangyuan were being delayed—"refrigerated"? Some from C. P. and Dr. Clarke had taken twenty-one days although the bus *came daily,* a matter of only thirty miles.

At length they got the little one quieted and to bed, then Father and Mother descended to the kitchen and the trunk, knelt down and prayed. They asked God what to do. The thought came, "Write an open post card of what medicines you have in the house. Tell Dr. Clarke her symptoms and ask him to please advise." An open post card would carry less suspicion. *Within four days,* and while they were actually down on their knees praying that the answer from Dr. Clarke would come through quickly, came the open post card with the doctor's instructions. This was the only day out of all the days of trial that the postman came before breakfast. And baby Lilah pulled through.

It was a real test to the anxious parents but *their peace of heart held.* The "best wine" of delighting in His will did not fail them throughout the heat of this experience.

Thus the summer of 1952 passed with one flutter of get-ready-to-go followed by the familiar silence.

Autumn had come and Felix's monthly grants of their money were getting impossibly small. If they must spend another winter in Hwangyuan, what would they do? The original three million which the Shanghai bank had sent them and which Felix held, was truly shrunk to a pitiful size. The question faced them—what should they do? Communist policy obviously was to move a foreigner only when he became a public liability (e.g., when his money was all gone). Felix had not asked them if they had other funds elsewhere. As a matter of fact they had! The Mission had left them a plentiful supply in the Shanghai bank. But why push this information, unasked, under Felix's nose? He would only dole them out starvation-allowance anyway and why prolong it? Just how much must they starve before he would grant them exit permits? Was it fair to ask Lilah to starve? Should they go without food and give to her? They both decided no. Her fate, if they died, would be worse than death.

Throughout all these vexing questions there was still peace of heart. They were merely seeking the mind of the Lord for today's action. But as the winter of 1952 set in, it was obvious they would not have money for coal. Now the poor of the land burned leaves and coal balls which were coal dust mixed with dung and water.

In September, 1952, Arthur decided that the time had come for him to do likewise. So getting a big sack, a broom, and a penknife, with little Lilah holding on to his finger and chatting happily, they sailed forth to join the autumn Poor Brigade. Every child, mother, sister, even grandmother was out on the hillsides sweeping up leaves, pulling up grass roots, collecting anything, everything that would burn for fuel for the winter. At sunset they would return with their loads and empty them into the cellar for winter storage. Arthur writes:

> I have been out day after day while the leaves have been falling, sweeping up leaves, picking up manure, gathering sticks, and cutting iris leaves with a pocket knife, collecting about fifty pounds a day. As a result we have been able to keep the stove occupied for our two fires a day to cook three meals, for ten or more days. It was good of the Lord to bring the shortage just at the time when the leaves were falling. . . .
>
> The impossible thing to us, is not that we should be supplied, but that we should be delivered from all our fears at the thought of another winter and have turned to face it (*not to run away from it!*) with peace and rest.

In September Arthur had applied to Felix for what he knew was the last of their funds in that man's hands. As he drew the money he said to Felix, "I have only this left here as you see. Please make arrangements for us after this is used up." But Felix did not arrange for anything. They had to go over two months on just that $37.50 and cold autumn months at that.

They were entering now on that period when for the second time Felix tried to starve them. How the Lord took care of them will be told in another chapter. But Arthur was forced to the making of coal balls. Dry leaves of course, will not yield a fire consistently hot enough to bake anything, but on top of flaming leaves these coal balls will catch and hold some heat for a short time.

And so he would select a seat out in the sun on those cold near-winter days and patiently mold coal dust and sheep dung with water from the river. For a gentleman to come in any contact with dirt, let alone manure, was unspeakably degrading in Chinese eyes. The melted snow-water made big cracks in his hands which were painful and yet he sat there day after day patiently molding them. The Chinese who had to pass him were really touched. He heard one of them whisper, "Dear me, dear me! Look at this! Look at this!" But he smiled cheerfully and every evening they had a praise and love-service to the Lord.

Only eternity will show what those "green leaves in drought" meant to the Chinese onlookers. Hudson Taylor once wrote:

> The converts of Paul saw that the apostle deemed it a small thing to *die* for them. . . . It is not mere preaching the Gospel which will do what needs to be done. . . . Our life must be one of visible self-sacrifice. There is much sacrifice in our lives of which the Chinese cannot know. God knows all about it, and we can well afford to wait for His declaration of it and His award. There is much that we have left for the Chinese which they have never seen. That will not suffice.

They must see self-sacrifice in things which they
cannot but understand. . . . We may reckon our
life by loss instead of gain—we may safely account that what we lack and lose and suffer are
our most prized facilities for bringing home to the
hearts of this people the glorious Gospel of the
grace of God.[1]

Through all those trials little Lilah was an asset,
not a liability. Hundreds in the homelands were
especially praying for the little girl *and your prayers
were answered.*

The time came when her milk money did not
arrive and for one week at least she was without
it—without meat, milk, eggs, or vegetables. Yet she
never complained; more than that she encouraged
her parents. One morning when sitting down to millet porridge with nothing on it, she dug in vigorously
at the same time saying, "When the Lord Jesus
makes the policeman give Daddy some money, then
I'll be able to have milk and sugar on my porridge."
There were no complaints from her about any of the
shortages, and she was filled with song. Only three
years old now, she had unconsciously memorized the
words of many of the hymns her parents sang those
days.

Arthur remembers squatting by the firebox of
leaves and coal balls trying to toast some bewhisk-
ered bread (with nothing to put on it). There were
times when he felt a kinship with the widow of
Zarephath. "She taught us that an empty barrel is
one of the most awkward loads to carry, apart from
God's help. No doubt she found that a barrel which
only kept a bowl of flour at a time was rather awkward!" And so that evening squatting beside that
leaf-and-coal-dust fire, trying to toast bread for a

---

[1] *Days of Blessing in Inland China.*

meager supper, the young father was feeling the awk-
wardness of it, when suddenly his little girl, sitting
beside him rocking back and forth, broke into song:

> In heavenly love abiding,
> No change my heart shall fear;
> And safe is such confiding,
> For nothing changes here.
> The storm may roar without me,
> My heart may low be laid,
> But God is round about me,
> And can I be dismayed?

They had no knowledge that she knew those
words! The father and mother looked at each other
and silently marveled. But on she went into the
second verse, sweetly warbling, to lift her parents
into floods of victory. *And safe is such confiding.*

> The old barrel [said Arthur], so ugly and
> burdensome! As we launched out recklessly
> abandoned to His will, the sea became a road,
> and the barrel bounced alongside like an old
> friend, buoyant as a cork . . . we are being
> satisfied with the best wine, so what more could
> we want?

Naturally Lilah felt it that the Chinese children
were not allowed to play with her any more. Wilda
writes:

> Lilah misses her playmates very much. . . .
> She loves her few books and [in summer] enjoys
> her sand-pile. Even as I am writing she is delight-
> edly initiating a new cart which Daddy has just
> made for her out of a wooden box and wooden
> wheels. The old one was too small and rickety.
> Often my heart is lifted up as she sits in her
> little chair, rocking vigorously and singing, *Lord,*
> *I believe, Lord, I believe. All my doubts are*

buried in the fountain. Praise the Lord for the little life which helps to brighten our days.

A further trial was to be added to those days. The Chinese on the compound were not "producing" adequately and so they decided to make noodles, dry and package them for sale. Tibetans and Mongols were especially fond of carrying such home with them so there was a good market for them. The Chinese cleaned out "the flea factory" beneath the missionaries' bedroom—that was a matter for gratitude. But they installed some very noisy machinery that squeaked in all the most nerve-racking keys.

Arthur writes:

> We are enlightened every night (or we were, for we got used to it now and go to sleep) from eight-thirty till after midnight, by seven hilarious spirits banging, shouting, laughing, grinding in the room underneath. During the day they manage to keep moderately quiet when there is no one out at that end of the house (!) but they positively shine as it gets dark and Lilah is put to bed. Needless to say they are the humble "co-operators" who have got going on a new run, and are trying to make the most of their opportunities to multiply filthy lucre. They have a machine down there for making noodles, and a carpenter's bench for making rollers to hang the stuff on, and a department for sieving the flour (nothing is noiseless!) and by the sound of it, a department for cracking weak jokes at the foreigners and then laughing at them. I forgot the mill for grinding salt, but the sounds are all so complex that it is hard to separate them. . . .

> We would like to thank you for getting the home groups praying for us. We have heard from members that they have been to these meetings, and have been praying for us. . . .

P.S. Please let the people know that I do most
of the writing here because I am the lazy one in
the family. Wilda has her hands more than full
trying to make old things grow up with the lassie.

Again later:

We have wondered a lot how much of the
details of our last winter's escapes and escapades
were really glorifying to the Lord, and how much
just produced a sigh for "the poor things." Then
as we are being led along a similar path this
winter, we hesitate before recounting details. But
we do want you to know that we still need earnest
prayer and worthy prayers (the prayer that is
worthy of Him who works all things according to
His well-pleasing), not the semi-hysterical prayer
that His long delays often lead us into. We are
SENT as sheep (without any degree of intelligence
or personal security apart from the Shepherd)
among wolves, *and we are proving the Shepherd's
heart.*

And so the green of a life secretly satisfied despite
outward drought continued to unfold before the gaze
of man. They continued to be a testimony of "trusted
to trust and not be offended." Of trust, someone has
written:

With cheerful faith thy path of duty run
God nothing does, nor suffers to be done,
But what thou would'st thyself, could'st thou but see
Through all the events of things as well as He.

CHAPTER TEN

God Takes Over Mother Hubbard's Cupboard

BY NOW (September, 1952) most of the Mission's members were out of China and so family concern ran high for the five in the far Northwest. Mrs. McIntosh and Miss Mary Milner had sent the milk money for Lilah until they had to leave, after which Mrs. Elizabeth Gould in Shanghai had taken up the good work. The Goulds had left the C.I.M. to go into business in that metropolis, deliberately hoping to be able to stay on as business people, and thus still minister for the Lord. (For this reason they were not reckoned in with the C.I.M. remnant of five.) Arthur wrote to them constantly and so they learned how hard up he was for shirts. Harry Gould was accountant in the office of Butterfield and Swire.[1] One day he happened to have a talk with his stenographer who was the wife of the manager of British General Electric. Harry happened to mention Arthur's plight in shirts to her and she immediately offered some of her husband's. It seems that they were preparing to leave for England and she had to dispose of superfluous baggage; her husband had had white shirts tailor-made by the dozen and she did not want to cart them home. Harry remembered that her husband was about Arthur's general build and size,

---

[1] A big shipping firm.

and so he gratefully accepted them for the ragged one in Hwangyuan. Thus we read:

> September 10, 1952. We have enjoyed mail and parcels from H. and E. [Harry and Elizabeth]. I think I told you the shirts had come through and were received with three cheers on all sides. We are better off than Seepy, for his pound of tea is still in the drain.[²] . . . We hope to share the fun with the boys next door.

And they did. There were enough shirts to give Clarence and Rupert some each. Wilda managed to get some common Chinese dye and colored them all blue, as that is easier to launder.

Arthur's letter goes on:

> With yesterday's mail there was a special from the blue (I suppose Switzerland can be called that?). . . . Truly we are humbled at the way the Lord lays the burden for prayers on so many who are so far from our normal sphere. . . . The Swiss parcel was a godsend truly. It contained three or four packages of desiccated soup and some compressed ovomalt cakes. Wilda cut these latter up into cubes about the size of bouillons.

But now Lilah's third birthday was approaching —September 16, 1952. She had never had a birthday party; her first year she was too young, and the second year her mother had been too ill. Like every Mommie, Wilda longed that her little girl should have a happy birthday, and so she set to work to plan one. Arthur writes:

> Wilda is using the material that wrapped up the shirt parcel to make a doll to replace the one that disintegrated sometime ago. Alas, I shall have to be the artist to put the face on. She has

---

[²] Still in the mail.

a Koala teddy, almost devoid of its hirsute cover-
ing as the ecclesiastical functionary in the domi-
ciliary edifice erected by John [the priest all
shaven and shorn in *This Is the House That Jack
Built*]; but that troubles her not a bit. Bunny runs
a very close second to Teddy at present; he was
made by Amy McIntosh two Christmases ago and
has no hair to lose. Then there is an oilcloth
duck—that's the family!

Now every party infers guests, playmates. As no
one was allowed to talk or play with Lilah, Wilda
used the toys as guests, seating them on the table,
leaning against the wall. Arthur made paper dunce
caps for each and for themselves. In a junk pile
Wilda had found some dye and one and a half birthday candles. Breaking the one candle in two gave
her the needed three short ones. For a long time she
had been saving the ingredients for a small cake
baked in a coffee tin. Daddy took Lilah out to play
while Mommie fixed up the room. Then Lilah was
brought in and fitted into her paper hat, while Mom-
mies and Daddy donned theirs. Ben was standing
outside where he could see them through the door,
so they went through a pantomime for his benefit
that made him laugh and understand. As Lilah was
marched up to the table, there the small birthday
cake shone under its three candles, the new rag doll
grinned delightedly at her; and Teddy, Bunny, and
Duckie sat in the dignity of their new hats, watching.
"Happy Birthday to You!" they all sang, then sat
down to cake and weak tea.

They had just finished when the Lord did the over-
abundantly. There was a knock at the door. On
opening it, there were two of the Russian's children
come to play with Lilah! They had not been there
since June; and they never dared to come to play

again; and they did not know it was her birthday. A gift straight from our heavenly Father! Every Mommie will know why tears of gratitude wet the cheeks of Wilda as she heard her little girl's cry of delight—playmates for one whole afternoon.

Wilda found such fellowship, those days, in this word from Oswald Chambers: "The things that make God dear to us are not as much His great big blessings *as the tiny things;* because they show His amazing intimacy with us; He knows every detail of our individual lives." And the little birthday party which she had planned and which He "embroidered" was one of the tiny things which made Him dearer than ever.

September is the month when Chinese and Buddhists celebrate the moon festival and make a certain kind of cake and rice bread. On the compound living near them was an old Tibetan lady, perhaps a hundred years of age, pensioned by the Plymires. Sick, almost blind and toothless, she must have heard the Chinese talking about how poor the white man was now. We do not know; maybe it was just the prompting of the Lord, for she was somewhat deaf. At any rate, one day Wilda heard a sound at the door and there was this dear old soul. She had *crawled* up the steps to the kitchen, pulling herself along weakly. In her hand was a package wrapped in an old dirty cloth. She held this out to Wilda mumbling something about, "Thank God for the pastor," then she turned and crawled back to her own room and bed. A few weeks later she died. But when Wilda opened the cloth, inside were five or six cakes of steamed bread with bright red and yellow marking on them. They could be baked to kill the germs and were good nourishing food.

One of the principles of the China Inland Mission

is that its members do not go into debt. If money for a purchase does not come, that thing is not bought. The Chinese were great money-borrowers and it would take some time for them to believe that the white missionaries would actually go hungry rather than owe money. When they did see it, it made a great impression.

By this time Pastor Jen was having to do trade with a small stall on the street. One day in passing Arthur he whispered. "If there is anything on my stall you need, just take it."

The Russian Christian also had a stall and among things he sold salt. The day came when Wilda's supply was so low that Arthur felt he must use a few of their precious pennies to get some more. Accordingly he went to the Russian's stall and ordered just a very small amount. The dear Christian man gave Arthur one deep look, then tipped up his salt tray and deliberately sent a cascade of it into Arthur's basket—and refused any payment. It was not possible to thank him properly in so public a place, for he might be caught helping the hated imperialist, of course. But this was joy to Arthur and Wilda, which they did not soon forget. Millet porridge without milk or sugar is one thing; without even salt what would it have been! It was not asked of them. The Lord had put some salt into Mother Hubbard's bare cupboard.

In the meantime Arthur swallowed his pride and went seven or eight times to Felix to beg him to make some provision for them. He hoped, of course, since Felix held no more of their money, that exit permits would be issued to them, but not so.

Arthur writes:

Sorry for the long silence, but having been over Niagara in a barrel, down the rapids and through the whirlpool, we had little conveniences for letter writing. The bust-up, or showdown, came with my application on October 2 and 4. I was told to write to Clarence and get dough from him.

Clarence Preedy, as C.I.M. local secretary to Kansu personnel, had previously drawn a good supply of money from Shanghai for all their use, and that money was in Sining, but as Arthur expressed it, it was "towed into Iceland."

But in the meantime the Feather Curtain of God was softly warding off the planned starvation. One evening there was a knock at their door. When they opened it, the Russian's little girl stood there with a basket. Quickly she opened it, took out about ten pounds of meat, thrust in into their hands and ran off. In the days before intercourse was forbidden, she had been accustomed to come and play with Lilah, so her entrance into the compound would not attract much attention. They had not had any meat for several weeks—oh, how good it tasted! Wilda writes:

> Truly a miracle in every way have these two weeks been. The milk supply was cut, but in the Lord's mercy, what little we were able to get proved *richer* than we had been getting for a long time; so that we could water it down for Lilah, and the cream so thick that we still had butter! We had not been really hungry, and the weather has been warm right through so we didn't need the heat from the stove. How wonderfully faithful the Lord has been! He has been our strength and refuge in a very real way.

A little help came from another source. Clarence Preedy and Rupert Clarke, knowing how low things were with the Mathews' family, had sent them a parcel of millet, raisins, and sugar. These Wilda carefully portioned out, three raisins each were "dessert" for some time! But the time came when there was no fuel to cook the millet. Again we quote Arthur's letter:

> We boiled up several large crocks of water while we had the wood [all drinking water had to be boiled, of course] and on the last night a saucepan full of millet, so that if the money did not come we would at least have cold food and water. Daily I was inquiring at the bank for the remittance slip, keeping back our last post card to inform the neighbors [C. P. and Dr. C.] if nothing came of their efforts; but the one week which it usually took to come through lengthened out. Nothing came. Finally one night just before closing, I called again, but was met with a shake of the head. I turned and went out into the street to go to the post office and mail that last card, but I had not turned the corner when I heard my Chinese name called. I went back into the bank, and they handed me a slip for a minimum remittance to carry us along until the Sining authorities could make their inquiries about us. Next morning . . . I was able to draw the money.

That was the morning that they had expected to begin eating cold food! They never had to. Arthur was able to buy fuel, so that with the gift of raisins and sugar, they had a nice warm meal. The Feather Curtain had once more fallen in time to shield them.

Mr. Preedy and Arthur both had tried to tell the Sining police that Hwangyuan police were persecuting and would never hand over the amount of money estimated and needed. Eventually this was to produce results, but in the meantime, they "must investigate."

Winter was now definitely on its way and they saw they would probably have to spend it in Hwangyuan

again. Wilda was nonplussed how to provide for
Lilah. She was out of shoes. Leather ones, for
traveling home to America, had been sent from Hong
Kong, but she could not wear those in snow and
slush, they would produce chilblains. Everybody
wore Chinese wadded boots, made by Chinese
women and obtainable on the market. But there
was not enough money to buy any, and Wilda was
forbidden to talk with the Chinese women, or she
would have inquired how to make them and tried
herself. Her only resource was prayer; so down on
her knees the dear mother went.

Again the answer came with a rap on the door.
And again it was the Russian's child who stood
there, holding out a dirty-clothed bundle, then hurriedly ran off. When Wilda took it inside and opened
it, it contained—*wadded shoes!* A little on the big
side for Lilah but they could be padded and used.
This gift was the more touching because that Russian
Christian had five children of his own, and at this
particular time, his wife (family shoemaker) was
sick.

"My measure is full, now that I have received at
Epaphroditus' hands what you have sent. It is no
mere gift to me," is Dr. Way's rendering of Philippians 4:17. Truly Wilda felt just like that; it was no
mere gift, it was a miracle.

"Your generosity is like a lovely fragrance, a sacrifice that pleases the very heart of God," renders
Phillips of Philippians 4:18. There were other trees
of the Lord, sprouting green in drought, besides
those of the American and Australian missionaries.
And how it blessed the hearts of them all— this one-
ness in Christ.

But another great need Lilah had for the cold
weather was a new snowsuit. The scarlet one she

had come in as a baby of thirteen months had been enlarged to its limit. The hood was still possible, but nothing else.

About this time a parcel from Hong Kong arrived. Missionary friends had heard that some parcels came through and so had tried this one. It contained a dark blue sport shirt from Marvin Dunn, and the Gunzels had put in some wool underwear and socks which they no longer needed. The moment Wilda saw the shirt she gave a cry, "There's Lilah's snow-suit!" and pounced on it. Arthur had the others anyway and this with its straight bottom edge was just right for a coat. She put pleats in over the shoulders, and slipping it on Lilah, it came just to her ankles! It had to be wadded so it needed to be roomy. They had a baby's old blanket worn too thin for use, but part of its wadding was still usable. They ripped this up and got enough camels' hair to wad the snowsuit. For a lining, Wilda ripped up an old faded cretonne cushion cover—and behold the snuggest of wadded coats! She enlarged the original mittens from the belt which gave her a two-tone pair of mits—quite the modern style. Later when money came, they were able to buy some fur on the local market, and for the trip out sitting unprotected on top of a truck in icy weather, little Lilah had also a warm fur collar to nestle into. This, to the dear mother, who had again and again ransacked her bare cupboard, was like a miracle.

Arthur, proud of his wife's ingenuity, writes:

> The shirt Marvin sent was definitely of the right color and suitability for present needs. Wilda has turned it into a wadded coat for Lilah, and she catches everyone's eye as she waddles down the street in it—the perfect football! I am sure it will change next year's fashions for the young (!).

Fortunately she does not understand all the exclamations that follow her down the street. "Oh this baby! Doesn't she pull at your heartstrings!"

Lilah was allowed to go with him to draw water (she carried a tiny tinful), and perhaps go shopping once in awhile. Then Arthur goes on to describe Lilah's favorite Sunday evening song. Each Saturday night on going to bed she would say, "Tomorrow is Sunday and we sing 'Peace! Peace!'" When the time came, she would sit in her little chair in the kitchen, rock, and sing happily:

> In Jesus for peace I abide,
> And as I keep close to His side,
> There's nothing but peace doth betide,
> Sweet peace, the gift of God's love.
>
> Peace, peace, sweet peace,
> Wonderful gift from above;
> O wonderful, wonderful peace
> Sweet peace, the gift of God's love.

Surely that testimony from baby lips blessed her dear Lord, even as it often fortified the hearts of her earthly parents. "How good to teach our children the 'meaty' songs and hymns of the church!" Arthur has often urged: "Let us fill their memories with words that carry deep heart-experiences and rest."

By the middle of November the little advance-bit of money from Sining had been used up, and once more Arthur had to plow up the road to Felix's office. He was wondering if a hint to let them exit would be wise. But he was only shouldered off. "We are looking into this; we'll let you know."

Two more days of silence. November 17, Arthur went again. A young policeman was on duty.

"Now you know," began Arthur, "we don't want the money so much as the pass to go!"

"I've no authority to grant road-passes," growled the sentry.

"But I was told a year and a half ago," persisted Arthur, "that the Central government *had* granted us permission."

At this word, out dashed Felix himself "like a hurricane, swearing mad." After him rushed out about twenty policemen all ready to bait the hapless victim. Arthur's knees knocked against each other so that he had to stand on one foot and then on the other to steady himself, but he did not flinch.

"Well, what do you want me to do?" he asked Felix.

"Write to your church in Sining and get them to send you money—and don't you ever come here again!" shouted that mighty one with foul curses.

Arthur called back, "I will, and I'll write to Peking too!" But the flashing vision of the prison inside the gates prompted him to apologize and retire as discreetly as possible.

Back home to Wilda he went, but for hours afterward he was still trembling. "I'm just never going back to them," he declared, and she in sympathy agreed that he should not.

"Hudson Taylor said that we could move men through God by prayer alone," went on Arthur.

"We will do that. But let us also write the Chief of Police in Sining and tell him how you have been treated. Enclose it in a letter to Clarence. C. P. will see that it gets right into his hands, I am sure he will."

This they did. And Mr. Preedy was as good as they trusted he would be. The Chief of Police read the account and then looked up.

"Did they really do that—at Hwangyuan?"

"Yes, they did."

"Well, I promise it won't happen again."

"The Mathews' family are out of fuel money, food money, and clothes money. No estimate all year has been granted in full."

"Send him half a million now, and we will see about the rest later," was his answer. Clarence, delighted, wrote them this and they waited expectantly. They waited and waited, but no bank summons came.

Ten days later it was a snowy blustering morning. For some reason Arthur was up early and drawing water from the river before breakfast. He wondered if Sining had sent the money *to Felix* and if he should try to go there again. "I'll put out a fleece," he said to himself. "If the Russian is at his stall so early, then the Lord does not want me to go up." He looked and—the Russian was there.

They sat down to breakfast and then had prayers. Wilda prayed first and Arthur heard nothing that she was praying. For inside him a voice kept whispering, "Go once more. Go once more."

"I've just told Wilda that I had a fleece which said not to go," he argued with that voice. "She'll think me a queer fellow who changes his mind in three minutes." But the voice insisted—"Go!"

When Wilda had finished her prayer, Arthur said, "Wilda, I feel I should go to Felix again."

"All right, dear," she replied. "You go and I will stay here and pray."

So in fear and trembling Arthur set out, slushing up along the edge of the snowy streets. As he came to the familiar gate, there was a new official standing there whom he had never seen before. He held a book in his hand from the pages of which protruded a slip of paper.

When he saw Arthur, he said, "Who are you and

what do you want?" But even as he was talking, his book fell open and Arthur saw the slip of paper; it was his own estimate-application, made two weeks before! Surely this was the Lord.

With new confidence our ex-major straightened up and said, "My name is Ma-liang-chen from the Gospel Hall. I put in an application here to draw some money and was told never to come back again. But I have no funds left. What am I to do? My application is there, in that book in your hand."

The stranger looked surprised; pulled out the slip and read it.

"Wait here," he said. In ten minutes he was back again with the police permit stamped for the bank. Arthur lost no time in going after that remittance! Then on to the market. *Within half an hour after leaving Wilda* he was back again with bread, eggs, meat, and milk! And still some money left. For three weeks they had had no meat at all.

Shortly after that he had another summons; Sining police had released to him one million for food, one million for fuel, and 800,000 for other needs. An avalanche it seemed—and just before the Christmas season Arthur wrote:

> The cellar has not looked as it does now for two years. . . . With the descent from the walk-by-faith to living-with-a-cellar-full I suppose there's a lesson hiding somewhere for us to learn!

Wilda writes:

> Oh how we praise the Lord for this answer to prayer . . . we're singing Hallelujah! . . . Lilah wants pears and candy. . . . Arthur and I both long for sweet things and eggs and milk. This noon Arthur said he was to have five eggs for breakfast! And I'm going to make a batch of

candy. . . . We can now buy shoes for Arthur
(I have good wadded ones but his are in a dread-
ful state) ; and we will buy a sleeping mat for
Lilah . . . [and so the joyous planning ran on].

The men at Sining were not forgotten. Wilda
made them fudge, and cookies and all sorts of good
things, wrapped them up as a Christmas parcel and
mailed them off to Clarence Preedy and Rupert
Clarke.

We have been on the receiving end so long
[she wrote] that it was a Christmas joy to be able
to *give* someone something!

Earlier Dr. Clarke had baked them a fruit cake
which was to be for Christmas; but when the parcel
from the Mathews' household arrived both he and
Mr. Preedy had been so reduced that they had nothing left to eat but beans! And so the Lord played
checkers, so to speak, with the bamboo curtain, and
saw to it that each little home had something special
for His birthday. The story of how they looked out
for one another is sweet. Dr. Clarke had begun it all
with his cake; then came the wonderful treat from
the Mathews' family—cake, cookies, fudge. Now
C. P. felt he was the only one who hadn't given
anything! What could he give? Oh, yes, he did have
something.

Months before he had seen two pounds of coffee
in a pawn shop. It was the coffee which Arthur
Mathews had sold when thinking an application for
an exit permit would soon be followed by the exit!
Mr. Preedy did not tell them he had redeemed it but
thought he would surprise them when they passed
through his station on their way out. The Mathewses
and the McIntoshes must pass through Sining. He
would open a pound for each, and surprise them with

a drink of real coffee! For the McIntoshes it had worked, but the Mathews' family still had not come. So C. P. wrapped up this last pound of coffee and sent it off to Hwangyuan; Arthur got it, said not a word to Wilda, but hid it until Christmas morning.

While Wilda was dressing Lilah for breakfast in that pantry nook, Arthur said he would make the toast for breakfast, and proceeded to dig out the coffee and make that too.

Soon a delicious aroma was filling the air, and Wilda sniffed wistfully. Was she getting queer, and imagining things? She'd better confess it.

"If I didn't know better," she called from behind the pantry shelves, "I'd think someone was making coffee!"

"Maybe the toast is burning or something," mumbled Arthur, trying to keep the secret until the family had gathered, but round the corner of the pantry shelves she darted, and there—on the table a pot of coffee!

"Merry Christmas from C. P.!" went a glad shout! And what a wonderful day followed! But let us hear it from their own lips. And to do so we must back up a day, for the happiest gift came on Christmas Eve from their heavenly Father.

> The outstanding gift to us for Christmas, 1952, was that *the Lord removed Timothy* on December 24. Off he went to Sining. After that Ben could talk to us some and even the pastors spoke occasionally. [No spying eyes watching their gate; no ear alerted to every sound. Oh, what a relief! And only the Lord could have timed it so perfectly.]

> On December 25, Lilah, all agog for Santa Claus before daylight, was a far better setting for a merry Christmas than the pitiful wailings for water every half-hour of the night last year.

One of the first questions was, "Daddy! What's the matter with you? Why don't you get up?" Then, "Daddy, are you praying to the Lord Jesus that Santa Claus will come?"

Our rose bush we have kept green so that was our tree, and it was piled well with presents for her. [Mommie had sat up sewing for quite a few nights before.] Cloth jumbo, and a clown (also cloth) took first place; then booklets, transfers, hankies, a ballon puppy dog, etc.

A friend called Winston came to the door later that morning with sweets for Lilah and a celluloid man.

Ben gave her a toy with a heavy bottom which you could not knock flat.

Then Christmas night, another kind of gift, from the One whose birthday it was. This is what happened. Timothy away, the local shepherd voluntarily came to the door to wish us Merry Christmas, and to tell us that the church was *packed with outsiders* and the few believers, who were met together for singing and the Christmas message. But I'd better stop numbering our gifts, or you will get dizzy.

What had packed that church with heathen, living under Communism? *What we lack and lose and suffer are our most prized facilities for bringing home to the hearts of this people the glorious Gospel of the God.* They had seen green leaves in a time of drought; they themselves were dried up to the point of cracking. What made these Christians able to stay uncomplaining, smiling above their patched clothes, and despite their growing thinness? How did they stay alive when Felix had done his best to starve them? They knew the power of Felix. This was the service which God had planned for His children when He deliberately brought their feet into the net.

One more little touch of the Feather Curtain of God. The letter says:

> The day after Christmas a wonderful box came through the post office—three chocolate bars, books, a toy wristwatch that would wind, crayons and a color book for Lilah. *We never knew who sent it or how it got through. . . .* We had wondered if the Christmas sweets would all be a flop because Lilah had never had any before. But she did love that chocolate.

Phillips renders I Peter 2:10 like this: "In the past . . . no experience of His mercy . . . now it is intimately yours."

How very intimate was God's care of that bare little cupboard in that far distant corner of the world, at the edge of the Tibetan grasslands! And how very varied and unthinkable were the instruments with which He quietly filled or replenished it!

An English businessman's extravagance in shirts.

An old Tibetan lady, nearing death.

A Russian Christian family—four times; meat, salt, wadded shoes, and birthday playmates.

Loving, concerned hearts whom they had never met, in far-off Switzerland.

Chinese Christians—one of them a boy living by faith.

A discarded sportshirt from Hong Kong.

A Voice that said, "Go once more," when he had been cursed off the premises and told never to come again.

And those over and abundant Christmas joys: toys for the girlie; coffee for Mommie from a pawn shop and an unselfish fellow worker; a Christmas parcel containing chocolate from an unknown source. *Intimate?* Yes, *tenderly* so. . .

And the crowning joys, which no human being

could have wrought: the Judas-spy removed on
Christmas Eve; the chapel packed with Hwangyuan
heathen to hear the Christmas message.

On the far reef the breakers
Recoil in shattered foam,
Yet still the seas behind them
Urges its forces home;
Its chant of triumph surges
Through all the thunderous din.
The wave may break in failure,
BUT THE TIDE IS SURE TO WIN.

O mighty sea, thy message
In changing spray is cast;
Within God's plan of progress
It matters not at last
How wide the shores of evil
How strong the reefs of sin.
The wave may be defeated,
BUT THE TIDE IS SURE TO WIN

—AMY CARMICHAEL

CHAPTER ELEVEN

"Specious Promises of Release"

IN THE ELEVENTH CHAPTER of Hebrews—that
honor roll of heroes of the faith—comes this
verse (37) which Phillips renders thus: "They were
killed by stoning, by being sawn in two . . . and
then were killed with the sword."

Right in the middle of terrible martyrdoms (stoned,
sawn asunder, killed) comes this apparently mild,
little word *tempted by specious promises of release.*
It does not seem to match the other sufferings. And
yet no mistake has been made. The slow wearing
down of the human spirit is a species of torture which
communists delight to use and have found very pro-
ductive for their purposes.

Specious comes from the Latin *speciosus* which
means good-looking; and Webster's dictionary gives
two meanings. The first, *showy;* the second, *apparently,* but deceptively, *fair, just,* or *correct.* It
exactly describes the promises of release with which
Red officials tried to wear down the spirit of the
Mathews' family and others.

You remember that it was January, 1951, when
they first made application for exit permits. It was
March before the Kingfisher arrived and deliberately
insinuated to Arthur that they could leave immediately if he (Arthur) would just co-operate; that is,
act as a fifth columnist in India for them. *Apparently
but deceptively fair.*

After that there was silence for four months. Then

in Sining, the police told Clarence that the Mathews'
family would be leaving next, and after them the Mc-
Intoshes! As a Chinese Christian was coming to
Hwangyuan, Clarence sent this word on to warn
Wilda and Arthur to get ready. This was the occasion when they had hoped to get out in time to see
Wilda's parents. They packed everything, listed all
the items which they were taking with them in ac-
cordance with the rules, and even went to live with
the Chinese for four days so that they could be ready
in a split-second to go. They were never, on any one
of these occasions, told that it was a false alarm.
"Hope deferred maketh the heart sick"; they were
just left to infer by silence and indifference that it
was only a tantalization. *Tempted* by specious promises.

We saw that the first year of 1951, and up to
Easter, 1952, their spirits *were* tempted. They were
restless and unsettled, constantly watching the calendar, checking off the exits of the other members of
the C.I.M. family as they poured out of China—over
six hundred left in that first year. Always they
hoped, "Surely we must be next" and continued teas-
ings urged them on. For instance, one month after
Clarence's useless warning, Pastor Jen was approached by the Hwangyuan police. "Got some
foreigners down in your compound? Well, tell them
to get ready to go!" This was surely it? And word
came that the McIntoshes and Miss Mary Milner had
already left their stations and were at Sining, pre-
sumably on the way out. Not really; they were held
there four months, but at first that could not be fore-
seen. But no, no further word of exit after the message through Pastor Jen. Once in July, once in August had come warnings, and now in September came
a third. "The white people are being moved on!"

came a rumor. Clarence had been told that the
Mathews' family would go before the McIntoshes—
surely this was for them? But no. The Roman Catholic priest was summoned but they were not. And so
they were "tempted."

Then God dealt with them about *delighting* in His
will rather than merely submitting. And you remember that by this time prayer helpers at home had
begun to concentrate on them—the two things are
definitely linked together. Taking the yoke was
God's gentle message to them, rather than just suffering it. This made all the difference in the world,
for it lifted the strain off their spirits. It was again
the Feather Curtain of God, silent, mysterious, baffling to the communist because it was something he
could not reach; but protective and restful to His
children. They accepted the teasing promises to let
them go, no longer believing in them. They *abandoned* themselves to the will of God to stay on in
poverty, under humiliating treatment, and with
starvation constantly threatening them from without.
And they tell us that the peace of God never left
them. Their spirits were *not* worn down by these
specious promises, but grew strong, sapfilled, and
verdant.

"Patience is staying under, when you can't get
out," Arthur once said. "But meekness is staying
under when you *can* get out!" There is a vital difference there and it is related in essence to the feverishly hoping for release with the abandoned delighted-
to-stay as long as He planned. Oswald Chambers
once said: "There is a great charm not to *know,*
but just watch Him unfold His purposes." But it all
takes its course in the conviction that they were not
the victims of a mistake, but His children definitely

led by Him into a net. This gave the meekness to stay on and take it.

After their *"Best Wine Now"* experience, they were again "tempted." A year after their word to get ready to go, which was unfulfilled, Pastor Jen appeared at their door. By this time he had been forbidden to speak to them so they were surprised.

"Pastor Chin and I have just been to a special meeting of the police," he said. "The head officer said to me, "You have some foreigners down there at the Gospel Hall, haven't you? Well, tell them to reapply for exit permits.' So that is my message to you."

This seemed very plausible. Their money which was in Felix's hand, had dwindled and the next month they must draw the last of it. So they presumed as they were approaching the penniless state, *this* promise of release would be bona fide. They spent money to have their passport pictures taken, wrote out their applications and got ready. Only again to be met with silence. But the peace of God was theirs and never left them. Arthur writes:

> Truly we seem to be the world's worst or best at false alarms! . . Our time passes in hair-cut bounds. When I get a cut I wonder if that will be the last and then time bounds on to the next duty with an apparent "situation unchanged." . . . We were informed in a roundabout way that if we still wanted to go home we should reapply for permission. This we hurried to do, still not fully wise to the fact that this seems to be an idea of a joke in some people's minds. Another is to make us repeat every request for money and to keep us running uselessly and harmlessly, back and forth. . . .
>
> Guess people are wondering what it is like to

be OMEGA! [The last letter of the Greek alphabet.] He has reserved that place for Himself. . . . Only as we think of One able to cope with all that that means, do we find something to rest our hearts on. Isaiah 52:12: *and the God of Israel will be your rereward* is still as true now as it was when the Lord first gave it to us sometime ago, for this prolonged exodus. I am having a spell off from taking Lilah out, after her afternoon nap. . . . I do all my odd jobs outside in the morning, and then am free in the afternoons for writing. I should have the reach of a gorilla after all the water I've carried. Not having a pole, I carry it in buckets, and while the snows were melting the river was so dirty that I had to go quite a bit farther to find a spring—which meant about one mile round trip a load. We use about two loads a day on the average.

Wilda writes:

It is truly wonderful to know He has the blueprint and is following it to the dot. The other day it just flooded over me—the realization that we are prisoners of the Lord—even as Paul wrote. Kept here by Him for His special purpose. . . . I used to feel so concerned about the future . . . I can truly say that none of these things bother me now. He knows what is best and will work it out. If we want our way we not only spoil the plan but *in gaining we lose* (Mark 8:34-36).

And after all, how little these things really count! We've been one and a half years using tin plates, bowls as cups, tin cans for sugar container, salt cellar, etc.; washing our plates for the next course; using a saucepan for washing and using it again in getting a meal. No curtains, no bedspread; just nothing homey or pretty or attractive. I've longed *many* times that it be different (especially things for Lilah) but I've learned that these outer things though desirable are not *essential*.

And so the heart-victory held.

From August, 1952, they passed into those two and a half months of miracle gifts for Mother Hubbard's cupboard, and then the great release when their financial problems were transferred from Hwangyuan police to Sining police. But even here, exuberance was restrained. Arthur writes:

> In case you have not heard already, you will be glad to know that we have turned the corner, and now look to our local secretary [Clarence Preedy] for supplies. Alas and alas this does not mean that we can do without our little worm-act! We still have to perform. But even for that there is this gracious word, *Fear not, thou worm Jacob, for I will uphold thee.* [Arthur called this verse THE LORD'S SPECIAL FOR WORMS. His letter continues]:
>
> With the change there could be a possibility of better things, for being in the hands of the police at Seepy's end is a far more cheerful and hopeful prospect, for everything gets spoiled here. We have refused to look at this change for the better, for we look not at the things which are temporal; for as with Israel, so with us.
>
> He can make their enemies to pity them; and if He doesn't through this change, then we don't want anything but what He sends.

The happy, full cupboard Christmas, 1952, being over, they entered the New Year, 1953—their third New Year at Hwangyuan.

On January 8, in Sining, Clarence Preedy was told that he and Mrs. Mathews and Lilah were to get ready to leave immediately—Arthur and Rupert Clarke to remain. *And no money was given to any*

of them all that month of January! But no exit permit was given either.

Arthur writes:

> We got into another flap after Clarence's letter
> telling us that Wilda and Lilah would have to
> leave immediately. We had to pack to go sepa-
> rately; and go over our notes of two years; but
> we are settled now. "Water wears the stones";
> and some are skillful in the application of this
> particular sort of water-treatment. . . . This is
> the fifth unfulfilled promise!

But now the men at Sining were really very, very
low. You remember they had been low at Christmas
when Wilda's parcel arrived. Arthur had used up
their Christmas remittance to lay in fuel and food, so
they too had no cash to spare. In fact, when Lilah's
milk money came in the familiar envelope, they decided to let her do without milk for a week, and send
it to the two men at Sining. This led to a sweet little
Feather Curtain touch, but to explain it we must go
back chronologically a moment, in order to talk
about Ben.

When Timothy turned Judas and came to spy,
Ben also appeared to waver for a time. The communists, of course, say frankly that to tell a lie on behalf of the cause is a virtue; therefore, when they arrange a case against a missionary, false witnesses are
not hard to find. When their stories are made to
dovetail, a very plausible-sounding frame-up is the
result. This has shaken many fine Christian Chinese,
to the heartbreak of their maligned missionary.
Whether Timothy talked Ben over or not, we do not
know, but there was a period when Arthur and Wilda
prayed very anxiously for Ben. But the Russian
Christian had also taken him on his heart; he sought

Ben out, talked and prayed with him, and gradually Ben came back to his previous joy in fellowship with the missionaries. Token of this came one day when the Mathewses heard a rattling at their kitchen drawers and found a note inside!

Ben occupied the room next the kitchen, and in both rooms were built-in drawers which backed one another. Thus, with Timothy watching and listening to everything, Ben conceived the idea of pulling out his top drawer and slipping notes into the Mathews' drawer! Or even, if he could get a signal through to them, whispering to them through the drawer space when each pulled out their top drawer!

On the morning when they had sent Lilah's milk money to Clarence and Rupert, the old Tibetan lady arrived as per usual, her rattail-like braids rattling down over her shoulders and over her oily sheepskin gown.

"Don't bring us any more milk for awhile," said Arthur to her. "We haven't any money for it just now." But the old lady was slightly deaf.

"What did you say about the milk?" she shouted.

"Don't bring any more until we tell you!" yelled back Arthur.

"Why? What's wrong with my milk?" shouted the perplexed old lady. The pastor not buy milk for his baby! What was coming to pass?

"Your milk is fine," yelled Arthur. "But we haven't enough money just now." At last it penetrated the old Tibetan ears, and necessarily the ears of anyone else within the compound! Shaking her head with its many braids the old milkwoman turned away, muttering to herself.

But as soon as Arthur got back into the house, there was a rattling noise at Ben's drawer. On opening this they found one hundred thousand Chinese dollars (about $4.50 U.S.). "Your wife and child need the milk more than I do. I can live on potatoes," he said simply.

Wilda and Arthur were deeply touched. Timothy had been well supported by a Chinese lady who hoped to marry him! But Ben was living by faith; no one was behind him with regular support. When money was low he lived on potatoes, and they always knew when he had a special gift, for they could then hear him making noodles. Now Ben had an uncle who was a party member, and who had offered him a good job in the Red government, if he would just give up his religious notions! But Ben had said that he wanted to trust and serve the Lord like Hudson Taylor did. Illustrious Benevolence; when your parents gave you that big name, I wonder did they guess how early in life you would fulfill it! Just a few days before he had received a gift from the John Sung Bible Institute and this gift for Lilah's milk was one-third of what he had been sent. Remember to pray for this laddie, still living and serving the Master.

So Lilah's gift of her milk money to "Uncles" Clarence and Rupert did not mean that she went without; just one day was she deprived of her milk.

But more than that, Ben offered to help Arthur if Wilda and the little one had to go first. Arthur writes:

> If Wilda leaves me solitary, we faced the possibility of a far less free and easy C. B. [confined to barracks] or even Don C.'s predicament. [Don Cunningham was in prison for many long months. Then he refers to Ben.] The above-mentioned has volunteered, without being asked, to be our Onesiphorous (II Tim. 1:16). God bless the dear brave lonely soul.
>
> The ground may seem awfully dry, but that is

the ideal for God's *root out of a dry ground* (i.e.,
the cross) to blossom and fruit through the ages.
So such souls, even though seemingly remote from
active flower and fruit-bearing are the promise of
both. There are limiting factors in them, of
course, as there are in all of us. . . . I think
Hudson Taylor said, "God can't have the result
without the process." So the precious fruit needs
the long patience of the Husbandman.

A month of silence from the police passed, and the
Mathews' family were busy trying to get hold of
some of their money when, without warning, on the
morning of February 5 (1953), Felix himself appeared at their kitchen door! We'll let Arthur tell it:

DEAR HARRY AND ELIZABETH,

I'm almost too overwrought to write; certainly
I will have a job to write coherently, but will
trust you to understand.

Our money is in the bank; I am just waiting for
some co-operation as a result of my applications.

In the meantime I had a visit from Felix this
morning telling me to "inform my woman to
prepare to leave the day after tomorrow." Poor
little Lilah half-guessed that the permit excluded
me, and came up with a tearful, frightened look
on her face. She is not going to take it easily
once she finds out.

The man said, *"You* will stay here until after
the business of getting your woman away." So
guess what you like, but I am telling my people to
expect nothing and relax in prayer not for a moment.

We've been caught before by these prayer letups, and want to keep pressing the Throne for a
full answer. . . . Faith is the trained eyesight of
the spirit that can see and gaze into the invisible
world, just as our bodily eyesight does into the
visible.

I haven't received any travel allowance yet for Wilda, so I can only give her ten out of my thirty thousand for the month. I was promised five for Lilah, *not given;* and ten for travel, also not received. The Lord knows, though, and will work out the muddle.

We hope the Hong Kong authorities won't tell us to send Lilah back in again because she's on neither of our passports . . .

We don't know whether we'll be able to send a wire. Rupert has to eat, and I don't think Seepy'll think he can afford it till he gets his travel money. What we will send will be: FEMALES SINING MATHEWS, if Wilda and Lilah move there alone . . .

Sorry to bother you but we are out of cash till Felix gives me the chop on my application; and we only have one more stamp available—that which you sent us last.

Blessings on you both and on your ministry,
Loving regards,
ARTHUR AND WILDA

P.S. Packed, ticket bought, coolies here to take baggage, when word came to *stay*—so females still here.

This was the most painful of all. His precious few pennies spent on tickets (no refund was allowed), Wilda and Lilah all dressed for the truck, their boxes roped and a coolie stooping down to lift them, when Arthur arrived to say, "Stop! They refused to give you a road-pass."

Poor little Lilah ran into the kitchen, sat in her little chair and rocked back and forth sobbing with disappointment. *Tempted with specious promises of release.* It is sweet that the Lord notices our trials, and He does not list them as "small" or "but-you'll-get-over-it." He put this one down in his honor roll of Heroes of the Faith.

Arthur himself wrote:

> *Truly there is a place for gold where they refine it,* and the Lord has seen fit to appoint us to the place. May there be no unyieldingnesses in the metal; no spitting and sputtering in the process . . . Sorry we are such a sack of disappointments.

Wilda wrote:

> Thus ends the sixth time we've been told to go in these two years. We were neither one upset (been fooled too often I guess). Before long we felt it was the Lord overruling. Perhaps we can both leave together, at least from here—poor little Lilah cried, oh, so hard . . . but she got over it.

Needless to say it had not been easy for Wilda to face leaving Arthur alone, yet she dare not demur. It was because of Mrs. Clarke's reluctance to be separated from Dr. Clarke which had enraged the communists so that they put him into prison for three days to punish *her.* Wilda knew that so she dare not show her feelings to anyone but the Lord. In His presence she had bowed and let out her heartache. She says:

> One night I lay pleading with the Lord to let us go together, but the next morning I was confronted with Romans 9:20, 21: *Who art thou that repliest against God?* Or as the margin says, *disputest with God. Hath not the Potter power over clay?* As I faced it squarely, all I could do was to bow my heart and head and say, "not my will but thine be done." . . . What a comfort and help to be able to just leave it all with Him!

But how wonderfully and aptly the Word had spoken to her need. So there was heart peace. And yet it was not possible to escape a certain amount of suspense. Both Arthur and Rupert Clarke had serious charges against them now. False ones of course but *murder*. Three of the doctor's former patients who had died were now charged against him as the responsible agent in their deaths. Arthur was kept on tenterhooks wondering what they would finally produce against him.

But now after this sixth exit-tantalization they waited nearly a month before the police paid any more attention to them. During that time they were eating into the good food supply which Wilda had hoped to leave for Arthur, of course. Then—but we will let Arthur tell it:

On Sunday, the first of March, a bloke (or tramp, or possibly a budding policeman?) walked into the yard and informed me that "the woman" with the child were to leave the next day. I suggested that maybe she'd get along better with a road-pass, and that without a pass I could not see my way clear to buy a ticket. So he told me to report Sunday at 6:00 P.M.

When I got there I was asked whether I'd bought the ticket. So I quoted their Chinese proverb, *ih hwei seng liang hwei shuh* (first time got stung, second time know better). . . . Perhaps they thought that last time I was too zealous in buying a ticket before I had a pass. I was ordered to report in the morning.

As I was on my way home, a group of blokes (or tramps, or budding what-ever-you-call-them) joked as I passed them. "He won't buy a ticket. Ha! Ha!" So I knew that was a joke somewhere in the offing, even though I could not see it.

Monday morning after packing I reported— bright and early. Another man came past and asked if my wife was leaving that day. I told him it was up to them. I wasn't in the position financially to throw away money on a ticket without some assurance that I'd be able to use it. Then another came out and told me to buy the ticket that afternoon and to report Tuesday morning when I was ready to take the family to the bus. Seeing that tickets are not sold until 11:00 A.M. and the truck leaves at twelve, I thought the request rather out of order. But with a lot of running around, first after coolies, then to get the family, then to the authorities, eventually the truck pulled out with the worthwhile part of the Mathews' household on board.

Arthur then goes on, in very guarded language, to tell how Ben helped him. Ben later got into trouble with the police for this kindness to the hated imperialists, but Arthur could not have got through without his help. For he enlisted the interest and help of a Chinese family who were to travel on that same truck and who, of course, were enchanted with the little white child. Arthur writes:

> Needless to say I'd have been hamstrung without a co-operator!—the Lord bless him! He saw to the luggage, got it weighed in, and stood guard while I went to report ticketless. I had to explain that bus station was a good twenty-minute walk and that if I left it until the ticket was bought, there would be a real problem to get the police pass put through and get back again before the truck left. What a relief to see the pass!

> Lilah was happily waving her last balloon on the end of her chopstick as the truck pulled out, safe and content on the lap of a gentleman (there are still some of this quality) who with his wife were to see that Wilda and Lilah were looked after at the other end.

> I came back and spent the afternoon packing their beds out of the kitchen and cleaning up

generally. Am now settling down to what we hope is the last lap. The next thing will be to see if they think I can live on air! For if it had not been for Harry and Elizabeth I'm sure we would have been stranded. Seepy is well set up again, so Wilda and Lilah will be better served there than here. I am well off for books. Seepy has passed on about twenty, so there will be no monotony for a start. Also there is quite a pile of occupation in the mending basket!

If there is not the same *eagles' wings* quality to my letters, don't worry. *The mounting up* must be followed by *walking*—perhaps the harder thing to do. But the exchanged strength is available for both tasks.

I asked Arthur if the empty kitchen wasn't very lonely to return to after his loved ones left.

"No, the relief that they had actually gotten away was greater than anything," he replied simply.

March 4, 1953 Wilda and Lilah left Arthur at Hwangyuan.

March 15 they left Sining with Clarence Preedy.

March 24 they crossed Liberty Bridge into Hong Kong. Wilda wrote:

Is this Hong Kong? The tired little girlie asked the question again for the umpteenth time on the nine-day trip out from the far Northwest of China. Oh, how wonderful it was to her mommie and her "adopted uncle" to be able to say, "Yes, this is Hong Kong." We were crossing the trestle in *No Man's Land* between China and Hong Kong.

Only a few seconds before we had caught a glimpse of the Union Jack flying so gloriously free, and even at that moment we had seen the head of another *uncle* peering over a wall— one of our own C.I.M. missionaries, waiting to welcome us! . . .

It is almost impossible to express one's feelings of relief, joy, and happy gratefulness. Truly the goodness and mercy of the Lord had followed us all the way, and made many crooked places straight. Many times, one day by truck and the rest by train, we had seen the Lord definitely working for us, and how we praise Him!

Friends at Hong Kong wrote:

You will be glad to know that Mr. Clarence Preedy was reported to have been well, and very bright on arrival. Mrs. Mathews is thin but not ill, and little Lilah is a beautiful child—rosy, plump, and in good health!

Of course everyone wanted all particulars about the two left behind, so Wilda wrote a circular.

Before leaving Sining, Clarence was given the answer to some written questions. (1) Rupert is allowed to go out on the street to buy vegetables. (2) He has been given the bankbook and can draw money. (3) Arthur can get his monthly allowance through Rupert. (4) Rupert was given the keys to the place.

Rupert and Arthur are in good spirits and in good health, although both have a tendency to black out occasionally. At present both have fairly well-filled cupboards and money in hand.

In China Wilda had been asked by the policeman who examined her if she know why she was being allowed to leave?

"No," she answered. "Why was it?"

"You are permitted to leave because your money is finished. But your husband and Dr. Clarke are in a different category. They are criminals, and the Regime knows how to treat criminals."

This was all that Wilda knew about "the charge"

against Arthur. Of course it had been Red policy to hold the last members of a mission or organization, no matter who they were, and wreak on them all the hate and vengeance felt toward the group at large.

But we would like to point out that it was on the *seventh* promise of release that Wilda and Lilah had been freed. Seven is God's covenant number with Israel. It signifies completion or perfection. The enemy was allowed to tease and tempt with specious promises; thrust out and clutch back; but only until God touched his hand. When God said *enough,* his fingers fell open and the prey was delivered. *Delivered* as He had promised them that night when the King-fisher seemed to be winning (Isa. 49:25); and richer by far for having been *with God in the net.* The following poem had meant much to them during those days:

"Child of My love, lean hard,
And let Me feel the pressure of thy care,
I know thy burden, child; I shaped it,
Poised in Mine own hand, made no proportion
In its weight to thine unaided strength;
For even as I laid it on I said,
'I shall be near, and while she leans on Me,
This burden shall be Mine, not hers;
So shall I keep My child within the circling arms,
Of Mine own love.' Here lay it down, nor fear
To impose it on a shoulder which upholds
The government of worlds. Yet closer come,
Thou are not near enough; I would embrace thy
     care,
So I might feel My child reposing on My breast.
Thou lovest Me? I know it. Doubt not, then,
But, loving Me, lean hard."

—Selected

CHAPTER TWELVE

"Not a Hoof Nor a Husband"

Aᴺᴰ ɴᴏᴡ Wɪʟᴅᴀ had joined the rest of us, so to speak, on the shores of Malta, anxiously watching the last two distant little specks, as they bobbed up and down in the thrashing surf of the storm. Both were "husbands."

We did not have Paul's promise from God that *all* of our C.I.M. family would be saved, but we clung to that prayer of Mrs. Mason. She, like the prophetess Anna of old, has served God faithfully since her widowhood, in prayers and personal witness; and many of us felt that her cry, "Let not a hoof nor a husband be left behind," was inspired. At any rate many of the C.I.M. family took it up in prayer for these, our last two behind the Curtain.

Now as Clarence Preedy and Wilda came out, as soon as they reached warmer weather, Wilda had mailed back to Arthur their wadded clothing, hoping it would reach him. And again when they came to Canton, Clarence found that they would have one million dollars over; he had estimated for them what it had cost the McIntosh party to get out, but God had brought them through cheaper, it seemed. They would not be allowed to take any Chinese money across the border, so Clarence just mailed the million in a common envelope to Arthur—and they prayed. Both clothing and money arrived intact!

Arthur's first reaction, after his loved ones left, had been just intense relief that they would soon be out—

143

as we have said. But soon his own needs, of course, looked him in the face. Would they allow Rupert to send him any money? His supply was very limited by this time; but God's care of Mother Hubbard's cupboard still flourished. You can imagine his feelings when he opened that simple Chinese envelope and found one million dollars inside! (Did any other human being ever have such an experience! Of course, it was really only worth about $45.00 U.S.). And then the clothes parcel! He wrote jubilantly:

> Did I tell you that the clothes Wilda and Lilah left, together with those in recent parcels, have proved a very productive source of supply? I have been able to trade them for food and the score to date is: over two hundred eggs, [did you have five for breakfast, Arthur?] four hens, and bowls of milk galore. I feel happier now about the tax which I had to pay on the Hong Kong and Switzerland parcels. [He had been charged 180 per cent duty!]

But the weather was now getting into summer heat, with its multitudinous flies, insects, and diseases which they bring. Arthur was troubled again with a bad tooth and rheumatic pain in the back and shoulders, doubtless due to it. Both men longed to be together, as letters which came out to those watching on the shore indicated. Arthur wrote:

> I am seriously thinking of sending in an application for a pass to Sining for a few days in order to get dentistry done. The Hygiene Department here won't pull it, so no one on the street dare attempt it. It will give them added delight to hear I am suffering and still more to refuse the pass . . . unfortunately I cannot deal with the more-or-less gentlemen in Sining, but

have to do it all through the scruffy local speci-
mens.

Then in addition to this he got stomach trouble!
As he lay there for five days sick in bed, he wondered
if this were not God's provision to have Dr. Clarke
sent to him. He could not know that at that very
time Rupert Clarke was also tossing on a sick bed in
Sining wistfully wondering, "Perhaps this will make
them send Arthur here to take care of me."

But far away on the home coast Wilda and the
other prayer watchers received this news—each man
sick in his station; each praying for the other to come;
and then silence for a while. How anxious were the
prayers that went up! Would the two weakly bobbing heads on the surf really be engulfed? It was like
Horatius swimming the Tiber:

> Oft they thought him sinking,
> But just as oft he rose.

One moment it seemed almost hopeless; the next they
reappeared clinging still to some part of the ship. We
mean no comparison to the ship, but when the two
men came again in the line of vision they were always
clinging to the comfort and support of the Holy
Spirit—He upheld them always.

May 18 Arthur writes:

> Very pleasant change in application at this end.
> Rupert was able to send me a P.O.M.O. [post of-
> fice money order] so I'll be able to draw my
> share without having to see Felix. All the same,
> the granting of another month's dough always
> has a *hope-shattering* effect. I felt it worse last
> night . . . but this morning Jeremiah came to
> my rescue again (9:2). The *Devotional Com-
> mentary* says: "He sighed for release, but he

stayed; the moan of his soul increased the worth
of his loyalty to his task."

When the "hope-shattering" money allowances
came each month, did the *best wine* cease to flow?
We know that that is just the time when it gets richer
and sweeter, although only the person who drinks
may know it. I have found it interesting to note how
times of loneliness and sorrow have so often turned
the child of God to that little-read book, *The Song
of Solomon.* It was during the days of his imprison-
ment that this song came to mean so much to Samuel
Rutherford; it was during a heartbreaking experience
that it came to the life of Hudson Taylor, and he
later wrote his wonderful little devotional *Union and
Communion* upon it. And now again we find that
when Arthur was left behind alone, this is the por-
tion of his Bible from which he seems to quote so
often. He writes of how 1:13 was blessed to him.
*A bundle of myrrh is my beloved to me; and Mat-
thew Henry's Commentary:* "There is a complicated
sweetness in Christ, and an abundance of it."

Arthur says:

> There is a sweetness in Christ that will not be
> tied down to language no matter how extravagant
> the terms that are used. A *cluster,* that has the
> multicolor that Paul speaks of; turn it this way
> or that, put it in light or shade, hold it close or
> distant, there is always some new sparkle that
> fades not; something suddenly and overwhelm-
> ingly breath-taking; something pathetically stir-
> ring; something that moves over the heartstrings
> till they shiver with exquisite feelings that are al-
> most pain; or something that moves in the air
> around us, combining the comfort of the hover-
> ing mother-bird with the warmth and closeness of
> the sheltering feathers. All this and much more

is my beloved unto me. This is what I find in Christ. This is the answer of my heart in communion with Him.

By this time Arthur's letters were beginning to draw answers from the homelands; testimonies of blessing received through the lessons bravely learned. On one such occasion Arthur had been reading Song of Solomon 1:12: " . . . at his table, my spikenard sendeth forth the smell thereof." He saw the relationship instantly, and it was a deep joy to him. He wrote in April, 1953:

My spikenard just now must surely be a willing acceptance of *the fellowship of his sufferings.* Separation from home, wife, child, friends, and even service for Him. In sharing this with Christ today, my joy is full, my heart overflows. In this place and away from this place, He is unto me as *a bundle of myrrh* (the cluster) , the fragrance of which abides with me through my conscious hours. The joy of knowing that my spikenard sendeth forth its fragrance abroad to Him and to others outweighs the cost; in fact, makes the cost no cost at all. The service-scorched bride at last finds her rest at His table and in His acceptance of her spikenard.

Again:

One of our most precious verses is Psalm 34:4: *I sought the Lord, and he heard me, and delivered me from all my fears.* The determination to keep us on would cause another fear, if we did not flee to the above verse continually. [This reminds us of *clinging to some part of the ship;* he held on to the promises.] Our balance now stands at 860,000 which leaves enough to hold us through another two applications [which meant two more months]. Beyond that I refuse to think. . . .

> Looks as though we are in for a bit of personal
> attention along the way out. . . . Please pray
> for guidance for Rupert.

This last referred to rumors of a public trial on
the charge of murder for each of them—they did not
know the charge until almost the last moment. They
must pass through Lanchow on their way out. (Lanchow was the place where Dr. Clarke ministered in
his hospital, and Changyeh had been the station
where Arthur and Wilda worked before moving to
Hwangyuan—and also where that Mrs. Kao claimed
property and where Arthur's public trial threatened.)
These public trials were dreadful things, where the
populace were told lies and urged to a frenzy that
called for the execution of the accused. So the praying friends at home, watching this new monstrous
wave tearing over the sea toward the two little specks
on the surface, continually prayed that it would
"break" before it reached them.

Another month slowly passed, and during it Arthur
had a different kind of trial. He writes:

> June 14, 1953. The Devil seems to be center-
> ing his attention on Wilda's mail. I know that
> she is writing every three or four days, but the
> numbered letters that come are not consecutive,
> and three have been sad gaps. . . . When you
> don't feel too well, and have to potter around and
> keep wondering whether the medical book is right
> or wrong in guidance, then the days are inclined
> to drag. On Saturday I read Luke 22:37: *The
> things concerning me have an end,* and it has
> been a growing seed of comfort in my mind since
> then. . . . You will know that I am not trying to
> fix any time-limit; we've learned that it is not given
> to us to know. *It is not for you to know the times;*
> but we can fix the *facts.* And the fact is, there
> *is* an end. [It won't go on forever.]

We had a letter recently suggesting that as a certain husband was allowed through the Iron Curtain because of a wife's petition, so our wives should be given the hint. This of course demanded an answer, and I wanted clear assurance. The next morning in my quiet time I read Psalm 52:9: *I will wait on thy name.* The Lord spoke clearly to me from *Matthew Henry's Commentary* on this verse; he says: "There is nothing better to calm our spirits and to keep us in the way of duty (when we are tempted to an indirect course for our own relief), than to hope and quietly wait for the salvation of the Lord." That clicked very clearly in my mind and I would add to it Hudson Taylor's remark: "I have never seen the willingness to suffer and leave God to vindicate His own cause, His own people and their right, where the result has not been beneficial, if there has been rest and faith in Him."

This is a wonderful instance of the secret guidance of the Lord, and of His secret nourishment, *the hidden manna.* That growing seed of comfort, *the things concerning me have an end* was not a false hope. In less than one month Arthur was to be on his way out, hardly believing it was real. And in one month and one week from the day God gave that seed of promise, he would have reached the end of his testing; he was to be in Hong Kong and *free!*

We quote his account of how the end came:

Early one morning I had gone out into the yard to water my few vegetables. The only thoughts in my mind were that the parsnips were doing well and that soon I would have some fresh lettuce. So you can imagine my surprise when I looked up and saw a policeman, and the increased surprise when he told me to pack and be ready to leave for Sining in an hour! No other missionary exit

from communist China had been like this as far
as I knew. The usual routine was for a missionary to be called on at some respectable hour of
the day, told to get ready to leave, but then have
to wait weeks or months in irritating suspense
before actually being allowed to go.

I hurried back to the house, lit a fire, and
snatched my breakfast in between bursts of running up and down the stairs with things to pack.
[He took advantage of the officer's absence for a
few minutes to quickly swing all his remaining
foodstuffs and fuel into Ben's kitchen. Also he
slipped Ben one hundred thousand dollars and
said, "I am going home and you will be left. But
I am going to tell the Christians at home about
you, and they will be praying for you."]

One can imagine Ben's emotion. But then word
came to send on Arthur's luggage to a certain spot,
a police officer appeared and led him out after it.
His letter continues:

Later, sitting in the front seat (luxury of luxuries in China!) of the police vehicle, I said to myself, "This is the Lord's doing and it is marvelous."
From that first consciousness of the Lord's inter-
vention on my behalf there was no turning back.
The initiative was snatched away from my captors,
and it seemed that every attempt to brew up further trouble was met by God's: *Hitherto shalt
thou come but not farther; and here shall the
proud waves be stayed.*

He arrived in Sining about noon, and the first thing
was the examination of his belongings. They took
from him all papers: his Bible, his passport, and even
the wrappings of his razor blades! Then he was led
into the prison for the noonday meal and left there.
Sometime in the afternoon he was summoned, and,

as he was being conducted to the law court, he saw Rupert Clarke having his things examined. His heart leaped. Rupert had not seen him—would they be put together? Arthur gave a foreigner's cough; saw Rupert glance up and notice him, but they dare not exchange looks beyond that. Then Arthur followed the policeman out and into the law courts.

Here were seated the judge and secretaries ready to write down what was spoken. The sentry stood behind Arthur, and the judge read out the accusations.

"Charge one. Collaborating in the murder of Dr. Kao in 1936."

Arthur looked him straight in the eye and said, "In 1936 I was a student in Melbourne Bible Institute; and I did not come to China until 1938."

"Oh," said the judge, taken aback. "Well. when were you in Changyeh?"

"Not until 1948," answered Arthur.

"Charge two!" called out the judge, and it was read: "Arthur Mathews accused a girl to the K.M.T. of being a communist, as a result of which she was tortured and maimed for life." (A pure concoction of that Mrs. Kaos!)

"Charge three: In your journey through China from Chefoo, at Tsingtao, Kaifeng, Sian to Lanchow, you have spread sedition." (He was only a new language student then, with about six months' study! And had only stayed some three or four days in each place.)

"Charge four: Through photography and letter-writing you have proved that you are an imperialist." (Comments Arthur: "If you are cross-eyed enough to see the two together!")

"Charge five: You have seized someone else's property." (The C.I.M. had paid for many of the

buildings on Dr. Kao's compound, so naturally had sent the Mathews' family to live in one of them while they were working with the Changyeh church. This charge Arthur insisted was not his responsibility, but the Mission's.)

The judge then tried to bluff and threaten Arthur into signing a confession of these crimes. Arthur refused.

"Just put your name here," argued the judge, "and then you will proceed immediately to join your wife and child in America." (Possibly their reason for separating the little family—to coerce a confession.)

"I stand before God and before you," cried Arthur at the end of his patience and with the heat of indignation. "I deny all these charges. I will not sign."

"Well, then, we wash our hands of you," shouted the judge. "We'll send you to Lanchow and Changyeh and let the people decide what they want to do with you." That meant the public trial.

Arthur was then taken out to a small room where Rupert Clarke was also under guard; they were put in the back seat of a jeep but forbidden to speak to one another and driven to the prison. Arriving there they were put in separate cells; lights were kept on all night, and Arthur had other prisoners with him. He viewed the cell and found on the back of the door a placard. It read:

CODE OF PERSONAL HYGIENE

1. Wash your hands and face once a day.
2. Wash your body frequently.
3. Wash your clothes and your bedding.

But the walls were simply spattered with the corpses of bedbugs which previous tenants of the cell had squashed as they marched out upon them at night!

The next morning Rupert Clarke, with two Roman Catholic priests, was taken to the Civic Auditorium while Arthur was sent to a little room across the courtyard. By the loud-speaker he could hear their "crimes" being read out, and he naturally concluded that they were to be deported and he kept behind. Then to his surprise, a police official came running across the yard with a paper in his hand. Arriving in front of Arthur he read the previously recorded five charges, except that the first one had been changed to: "In league with the murderer of Dr. Kao in 1948." (Kao had been gone twelve years by then, of course.) The policeman shouted out Arthur's sentence: "EVERLASTING DEPORTATION!—to be put into immediate effect."

Arthur was rushed out into the courtyard where photographers were waiting, and the cameras clicked on all sides as he in his ragged clothes was marched into the police vehicle where Dr. Clarke and the Roman Catholic priests were already seated. These pictures, together with their accusations, would later be shown to the Chinese churches.

That day the truck took them to Lanchow to an inn. All four of them had to sleep together on the one k'ang (Chinese bed) and Arthur kept wondering what awaited him. The next morning they waited and waited but no summons to a public trial came. By afternoon he was still in suspense, when the shadow of a police official going across the courtyard jerked them all to attention. He came in and called them. "The time is now three o'clock. Your train will be leaving in about an hour. Have your bedding all ready to be taken on the truck."

Honest Arthur could not believe that this included him. "But I thought you were going to have a spe-. cial meeting for me?" he blurted out.

Rupert gave him a quick dig in the ribs and whispered, "Shut up!" The official mumbled something and went outside. Then all four of them were taken to a train and put in a compartment with four police guards.

The next morning at Tienshui they were told the line must be repaired, so they spent three days there in the railway prison. But the guards were nice to them and even asked them what they would like to eat. Rupert boldly spoke up for sweet and sour pork, and they received it! Twice it was served to them. This was for propaganda purposes; the Reds broadcasting that Americans drop germ bombs and gasoline bombs on defenseless villages; they bury people alive. But we, the Red Regime, treat even criminals like this, magnanimously!

From Tienshui they went by train to Hong Kong. Lying in his bunk that first night in which the train had bypassed all the trouble-centers (the prayers of those on the faraway shore that the threatening wave of a People's Republic might break before it reached them had been answered). Arthur's relief was too great to sleep. He wrote later of it:

> I feel that the Lord would allow even a Britisher a tear or two at the wonder of it all.
>
> Not having my Bible could not rob me of the comforts of Isaiah 31:4, 5: *For thus hath the Lord spoken unto me. Like as the lion and the young lion roaring on his prey, when a multitude of shepherds is called forth against him, he will not be afraid of their voice, nor abase himself for the noise of them: so shall the Lord of hosts come down to fight for Mount Zion, and for the hill thereof. As birds flying, so will the Lord of hosts defend Jerusalem; defending also he will deliver it; and passing over he will preserve it.*

That night lying in my sleeper, tears flowed on and off all night as I meditated on the little hovering mother-bird, the Feather Curtain of God; of the lion, roaring and fighting for His beloved Mount Zion; and the eagle—*as an eagle stirreth up her nest, so the Lord alone did lead him.*

Omnipotence could have swept away the enemy threats and oppression overwhelmingly, and we would have been satisfied. But how much more precious were the exquisitely tender ministrations of God, as our little mother-bird. How-much-more is an adjective that fits better than anything. Our how-much-more God!

Not only were the threats and accusations against us swept aside, but we were also given to see the extra mercies that might be called the exaggerations of love. First class food, sleeping accommodations all the way to Hong Kong, inn accommodation arranged, an afternoon in a cool teashop while waiting for a connection, a vehicle to ourselves from Sining to Lanchow, no luggage worries, no booking of reservations or standing in line for tickets, no responsibilities. The only disagreeable thing was that we were under guard all the way. We were not allowed exercise, and thirteen hours of sitting on wooden-slat seats can be tiring. It was funny to watch us all jump to our feet every time the train stopped! Just to stretch our muscles. But I am sure that all other exit-groups will go green with envy at our good fortune in being deported.

As the train went between Canton and Hong Kong nearing that long-looked-for Liberty Bridge, a verse from the Word came into Arthur's mind; *This is the day which the Lord hath made.*

The Great Manufacturer of Days [he wrote later in recalling it] had turned out a wide variety during the two and a half years of waiting after we applied to leave China. Some of the days we would gladly have skipped; others we could have liked to change; but He wanted to teach us to say at the beginning of every day: *This is the day which the Lord hath made; we will rejoice and be glad in it.* Having learned, though imperfectly, to say that very thing of days that had seemed miserable in their prolonged distress, it was not hard to say it on the day of deliverance! *The Lord preserveth the simple.* God does not look for a ready-made Hudson Taylor when He has some special work to be done. He looks for a man, preferably a weak man, and then makes him ready and fit for His work. What God did for Hudson Taylor He will do for the least and simplest of His children, if they will obey His voice and follow where He leads. This is my testimony.

The crowning point was their arrival PASSPORT-LESS at Hong Kong. Arthur said later, "We had no money so we could not phone Bryce Gray [C.I.M. secretary there]. But Father Patelli, who met the two Roman Catholic priests with us, put us through with them; sat us down to eat and drink; and then phoned Bryce to tell of our arrival. Do you wonder that we want to call our friends to *Sing unto the Lord for he hath triumphed gloriously?* Truly *He made their captors take pity on them.*"

Once over Liberty Bridge there was still a two-and-a-half-hour train ride to Kowloon where the C.I.M. quarters were. Arthur will never forget the moment when the German priest, seated on the opposite side of the aisle from him, suddenly pointed out the window as the train was slowing to a stop and cried, "There are your people!"

In another moment Arthur was into the aisle, out through the door, down the train steps and into the arms of the Family. Bryce Gray, Ken and Vera Price, Albert and Gertie Grant, Grace Potts, Marjorie Broomhall—just everyone who was free to meet that train did, of course. As the menfolk embraced the two gaunt and weary passengers, I am sure that some of the ladies were wiping away tears and thinking, "Not a hoof nor a husband left behind! *How great is the God we adore!* For the last of the C.I.M. family was *out!*

Cable wires were soon buzzing the news over the world. To America, to Wilda and Lilah. To South Africa, to Mrs. Clarke and her little son, just two months younger than Lilah. To Singapore, to C.I.M. headquarters; there, Mr. Arnold Lea sounded the gong, and as the members of the Mission dropped their routine work and gathered wondering what was the exigency for such a summons, he read out aloud the telegram: MATHEWS AND CLARKE ARRIVED TWENTIETH! Immediately there were thanksgiving and praise—and I am sure, very few dry eyes. . . . *and the rest, some on boards, and some on broken pieces of the ship. And so it came to pass that all escaped safe to land.*

Conclusion

Cloud of battle-dust inevitably dims the over-all picture of the campaign. The individual soldier must just trust the strategy to his commander and obey the orders given to him personally. In the spiritual realm the same is true of the disciples (soldiers) of Christ. But when the battle is over and the dust has settled, what has happened and the reason for certain orders will become apparent to even the common soldier. *In that day ye shall ask me nothing.*

It is clear to us now that the Lord's purpose in deliberately bringing His servants into the net was that they might live their message before the eyes of the weak and frightened little church. *What you are* speaks so loudly that I can't hear what you say. "All right," says the Lord, "then I will seal their lips. I will forbid their preaching. And will increase their drought until it is drier than that of the Chinese Christians; then through the lives of My servants I will prove that green leaves are still possible. And that my promise—*The Lord shall satisfy their soul in drought* (Isa. 58:11)—is for My children's use today."

Was the Chinese Christian falsely accused? So were Arthur and Wilda Mathews. Was he persecuted? So were they. Was he subtly reduced to poverty? So were they. Was he attacked by sickness and bereavement without much medical aid? So were they. Was he laughed at? jeered at? constantly humiliated? So were they? Was he tantalized by *specious promises of release?* So were they.

158

Was he forced to do menial work, thought very degrading? Much more Arthur Mathews. None of Arthur's social status among those who looked on was asked to mold sheep-dung and coal dust with their bare hands. None of that little church was forced to give up social intercourse with their fellows and live (so to speak) in silence. But the Mathews' family were.

And yet as trial was piled upon trial; as the ground (their human comforts) grew so parched with drought that it threatened to crack open, their leaf was still green. Every evening the sound of singing and praise to their dear Lord ascended. All the courtyard had heard when the father ordered the milk for the little one to be discontinued for lack of funds; yet that very evening, they not only sang but the song of praise had an exultant ring in it! (No one knew of Ben's secret gift.) And the next day the old Tibetan lady was recalled and the milk money was there! Had it fallen from Heaven? It most certainly had not come in by the door—that they knew. Did the God of Elijah really live? What more potent message could God have given these people? No wonder He deliberately sealed the lips of His servants, confined their hands and their feet, and then poured His life through them that the Chinese church might *see* and might desire.

Their clothes grew more ragged, and their food became so poor that the Chinese themselves were moved with pity. Yet still these missionaries sang on and taught their patched-clothes baby:

> In heavenly love abiding,
> No change my heart shall fear,

until she could sing it too. Was God wrong to do this? In the farthest, most inland part of that great land was God unfair to ask two corns of wheat to die to this world's comforts that others might see for two long years (not just two days: God gave them a good stretch of testing time) how *He is* sufficient for all these things. He sent them to serve by life and so sealed their lips. It was a much more potent message.

Andrew Murray has warned us how easy it is for the cares of this life to choke the Seed. He says: "The power of the world, the spirit of its literature, the temptations of business and pleasure, all unite to make up a religion in which it is sought to combine a comfortable hope for the future *with the least possible amount of sacrifice in the present.*" That describes the home church in 1956. But who knows when *the drought* is going to strike us also? Is it possible for any Christian to put forth green leaves when all he enjoys in his life is drying up around him?

We feel this question and its answer are worth sharing with you, hence this book.

> I will pour water on him that is thirsty,
> I will pour floods upon the dry ground;
> *Open your heart for the gift I am bringing,*
> While ye are seeking me, I will be found.

LUCY J. RIDER

Moody Press, a ministry of the Moody Bible Institute, is designed for education, evangelization and edification. If we may assist you in knowing more about Christ and the Christian life, please write us without obligation to: Moody Press, c/o MLM, Chicago, Illinois 60610.